SOCIAL WORK
A CALL TO ACTION
A TIME FOR REFLECTION
AND RECKONING

Linda Lausell Bryant

Philip Coltoff

Edited by Takako Kono

SOCIAL WORK
A CALL TO ACTION

A TIME FOR REFLECTION
AND RECKONING

Published and printed thanks to the support of
New York University Silver School of Social Work,
the Katherine and Howard Aibel Foundation,
Jonathan Aibel, and the New York Community Trust.

Book design by HansWorks.net

Linda Lausell Bryant and Philip Coltoff

Library of Congress Control Number: 2021908862
Copyright © 2021 by Linda Lausell Bryant and Philip Coltoff
Published in 2021

Printed in the United States

ISBN 978-0-578-89240-5

13 12 11 10 09 08 07 06 05 04 03 02   1

Publications:

Linda Lausell Bryant

Lieberman, L. D., Kaplan, A., Scholey, L., Kohomban, J., & Lausell Bryant, L. (2020). Strategic partners: Enhancing the ability of foster care agencies to serve the special needs of young mothers. *Children and Youth Services Review*, 110 [104808]. *https://doi.org/10.1016/j.childyouth.2020.104808*

Burghardt, S., DeSuze, K., Lausell Bryant, L., & Vinjamuri, M. (2017). *A Guide for Sustaining Conversations on Racism, Identity, and our Mutual Humanity*. Cognella Academic Publishing.

Lieberman, L. D., Lausell Bryant, L., & Boyce, K. (2015). Family Preservation and Healthy Outcomes for Pregnant and Parenting Teens in Foster Care: The Inwood House Theory of Change. *Journal of Family Social Work*, 18(1), 21-39. *https://doi.org/10.1080/10522158.2015.974014*

Lieberman, L. D., Lausell Bryant, L., Boyce, K., & Beresford, P. (2014). Pregnant Teens in Foster Care: Concepts, Issues, and Challenges in Conducting Research on Vulnerable Populations. *Journal of Public Child Welfare*, 8(2), 143-163. *https://doi.org/10.1080/15548732.2014.895793*

Lausell Bryant, Linda. *Perceived Social Support and the Path to College: A Comparative Study of Foster Care and Non-Foster Care Youth*, New York University, Ann Arbor, 2012. ProQuest, *https://tinyurl.com/279rv7ay*

Lausell Bryant, L. (2011). In Defense of the City's Sex Education Mandate. *Chalkbeat*.

Berberian, M., Lausell Bryant, L. and Landsberg, G. (2003). Interventions with Communities Affected by Mass Violence. In Straussner, S. L. A., & Phillips, N. K. (Eds.), Understanding Mass Violence: A Social Work Perspective. Allyn & Bacon.

Books:

Philip Coltoff

Preventing Child Maltreatment:
Begin with the Parent
Co-authored with Allan Luks,
Published by The Readers
Digest Foundation, 1978

Drug Abuse Prevention Study
Co-authored with Louise Murrey,
Published by the Child Welfare
League of America, 1979

The Challenge of Change: Leadership
Strategies for Executives and Boards
Published by JP Morgan Chase
Foundation in cooperation with the
Silver School of Social Work and
The Children's Aid Society, 2006

Crusade for Children: The History
of the Children's Aid Society
Published by The Children's
Aid Society, 2008

At The Crossroads
Published by John Wiley
& Sons, 2010

The Block: One Block in the South
Bronx, 1940s-1980s
Published in cooperation with
New York University Silver
School of Social Work, 2014

To the students, faculty, scholars, and university administrators who have had the courage to stand firm in the face of enormous threats to our democracy. And, to the advocates who remind us that we are inextricably linked and that none of us is well until all of us are well.

We would like to thank the Katherine and Howard Aibel Foundation for its generous support of our leadership work over the past 25 years. Katherine held a MSW from NYU and was a passionate advocate for children and families. We both had the pleasure of knowing Howard, who with Katherine, endowed the Executive-in-Residence and Visiting Professorship we have each held. We are deeply grateful to Jonathan, their son, who has been a wonderful partner to us after Howard's passing in March 2018. Thank you, Jonathan, for making this book possible.

Linda gratefully acknowledges Caroline Williamson, Executive Director of the B. Robert Williamson Jr. Foundation for providing the inaugural support to launch adaptive leadership work at NYU Silver and for her sustained funding over the past six years. Thanks also for her visionary and steadfast support of youth services agencies including Inwood House, which Linda led from 2005-2014. With her support as a then-trustee, Caroline championed adaptive leadership work for our agency as we navigated the impact of the Great Recession.

Linda also acknowledges Marc Manashil, MSW, MPA, the adaptive leadership expert who worked in real time with her at Inwood House to train her team and support her development in adaptive leadership. They continue to work in close partnership on the NYU and other initiatives to realize a shared vision for all concerned citizens to exercise leadership to advance justice and equity.

General Acknowledgments

A finished book, any author will tell you, is truly a collective effort. The author has the ideas and concepts, but the construction and organization of the book are more often than not the work of a solid editor. Takako Kono provided the structure and architecture for this book. She made suggestions, corrections, and fine-tuned the content.

Pat Beresford also offered many sound suggestions and along with her able staff, proofread the manuscript. The authors extend thanks to Hans Callenbach for the design of the cover and interior and his supervision of printing and binding, a complicated task.

A very special acknowledgment to the chief executives of social service agencies throughout the country who willingly responded to our questions and provided the insights to advance the knowledge base of our profession. A summary of their comments can be found at the conclusion of the book under "Reflections."

Dr. Michael Lindsey, Director of the McSilver Institute of Poverty, Policy and Research at the NYU Silver School of Social Work, responded to a series of questions by the authors highlighting the need for leaders to use their knowledge as policy makers and change agents.

Our thanks to the work study students and interns who helped type the manuscript, especially Megan Quitkin for her many suggestions and edits. To our spouses, Lynn Harman and Marshall Bryant, for their patience, thoughtful suggestions, and technical assistance.

Dean Neil Guterman was always available and served as a source of both information and encouragement. Lastly, the New York Community Trust, especially Natasha Lifton, always provided support.

Foreword by Dean Neil Guterman

Dean and Paulette Goddard Professor,
NYU Silver School of Social Work

We are living at a time of deep stress and distress. As I write, the COVID-19 pandemic continues to ravage communities, police violence against Black and Brown citizens continues unabated, anti-Asian, anti-Semitic and misogynistic hate crimes are surging, mass shootings are occurring at a heart-numbing pace, suicide is alarmingly too common, homelessness and mental health crises are overwhelming our helping systems...the long list of social problems seems only to grow. Our civil institutions like nonprofit and social service organizations, universities, schools, medical systems, and even democracy itself, are facing critical challenges. And at this moment, social work and social workers have become more indispensable than ever.

Professors Linda Lausell Bryant and Phillip Coltoff of the NYU Silver School of Social Work examine these major challenges of the day, and what they present for social work training, education, and practice. This book, *Social Work: A Call To Action*, looks at where our profession stands in relation to the major issues of the day. It examines how our profession's history, values, beliefs, and ethics require a democratic framework for its functioning without which the profession cannot exercise its responsibility to self-determination and individual liberty.

Lausell Bryant and Coltoff take a deep look at our policies, commitment to social action, and the education of our candidates to exercise the leadership necessary to move our profession forward. They look at hard questions of social reform as distinct from clinical practice, the influence of public and private money on the work that we do, the role of philanthropy, and the availability and quality of faculty committed to teach community organization and group work as agents for change. The authors also take an honest look at those who constitute our leadership core today—not only social workers, but attorneys, educators, and policy wonks—good people but not necessarily trained in our profession's knowledge base. They suggest new ways to effectively address these significant issues.

I commend professors Lausell Bryant and Coltoff for this undertaking. Their work is especially resonant with me, the faculty, and the students at NYU Silver School of

Social Work since we, as a total community, have been grappling with the issues of racism, inequality, and privilege in an effort to translate this awakening to a more effective use of self, sense of agency and advocacy.

I urge all faculty, students, administrators and practitioners to read this book; it will add to our understanding and appreciation of the great tasks before us.

Special Note from Ellen Schall,

Senior Presidential Fellow and Martin Cherkasky Professor of Health Policy & Management at NYU Robert F. Wagner. School of Social Work

Linda Lausell Bryant, PhD, MSW, and Phil Coltoff, MSW, both professors at NYU Silver School of Social Work, provide what they call a "gut check" to and for the profession in this powerful book and in so doing lay out both direction and prescription. They adopt the Heifetz and Linsky distinction between technical and adaptive challenges for leadership where technical challenges can be solved by what we already know and adaptive challenges are those that require new thinking, deep work and collective action. The critical work facing our nation and the world will be advanced if indeed the social work profession takes up the challenge these authors issue and re-centers adaptive leadership as a core part of social work teaching and practice, asking the questions inherent in adaptive leadership and insisting that the values at the heart of the profession enter the hearts and minds of all of us.

Universities are organized into schools and departments. I was faculty at and served as Dean of one of those schools, NYU's Robert F. Wagner Graduate School of Public Service, and as Dean led from the belief that the interesting ideas were at the intersection and that we needed multiple professions and perspectives brought to bear as we strove to address society's most vexing challenges. The authors advance that view as they call for a curriculum that crosses boundaries and brings together students from law, public health, education and public policy. Students and society would benefit greatly from this opportunity. Social work is both a profession, of course, and a perspective. That perspective, as developed here, has a great deal to offer and this book lays out all that and more.

Specal Note from Natasha Lifton,

Director of Government Relations at Trinity Church
Wall Street and former Senior Program Manager for
Human Services at The New York Community Trust

The COVID-19 pandemic and its economic fallout have laid bare the disparities in health, education, housing, and opportunity faced by people of color and poor communities across the country. In addition, the racial reckoning following the murders of George Floyd, Breonna Taylor and so many other Black people at the hands of law enforcement, as well as the insidious erosion of our democracy and rise of racism, anti-Semitism, misogyny, and xenophobia over the past four years have led us to an inflection point.

At no time since the great immigrant wave of the late 19th and early 20th centuries has the human services sector faced more challenge and opportunity. As Professors Linda Lausell Bryant and Philip Coltoff expertly delineate, the social work profession's commitment to advancing social justice and recognition of the humanity of all people uniquely positions social workers to lead human services organizations during these tumultuous times.

This leadership must embrace both direct service and social action—underpinned by the profession's values—to simultaneously address immediate needs and the drivers of systemic inequality. As such, schools of social work must ensure that social workers are fully prepared to lead by engaging impacted communities in the pursuit of justice and real change. This book provides a blueprint to do just that. I am deeply grateful to Professors Lausell Bryant and Coltoff for writing it, their years of exemplary service, and the opportunity to support their transformative work.

The Phil & Linda Story: Full Circle

LINDA

In early 1986, I was an idealistic 22 year old young woman with a Bachelor of Arts degree in Human Relations and a passion for work with people. I answered an advertisement for a case planner job at The Children's Aid Society's (CAS) PINS Mediation and Diversion program. Though the advertisement called for a Master of Social Work (MSW) degree, I was undaunted. My fluency in English and Spanish led the CAS team to give me an interview and I was hired as a Bilingual Case Planner. It was a dream come true and the beginning of a career in human services that has spanned three and a half decades.

Over that time, I have never regretted choosing social work and have always felt that I was working with a deep sense of purpose. At CAS, I was surrounded by a team of social workers with MSW degrees who were proud of their profession, committed to learning theory and practice, and dedicated to the people they served. I felt like I was with my professional tribe. It was there that I met Phil Coltoff, CAS's CEO. I was surprised that he took the time to get to know me as a new staff member, remembered my name, and seemed so accessible. He asked questions about the work, the clients, and their lives. Always ready with a story or a joke, he didn't behave in the distant, stiff way that I had come to expect from men in roles of authority. I had planned to pursue a graduate degree but was torn between the MSW and the MA in psychology. With support from my colleagues and supervisors, I pursued my MSW as a One Year Residency student, working full time at CAS and having new assignments to fulfill my field placement requirements. Within two years I proudly joined the ranks of professional social workers.

CAS invested in high-quality, consistent supervision and professional development for its team of case planners and supervisors. I was given an opportunity to present to the CAS Board of Trustees, a large, and at that time in my life, intimidating body. When I finished, I was standing a bit taller in my own eyes for having had that experience. After nearly 6 years working as a professional social worker, I was ready to move on to a new opportunity at Victim Services (now Safe Horizon), but my professional foundation was set at CAS and I always maintained fond feelings for the place where I began my career and the people who nurtured me.

Fast forward to 2007, by which time I had been serving for two years as the CEO of Inwood House, a historic youth development and child welfare agency that helped system-involved pregnant and parenting teenagers achieve strong educational, health, employment, and parenting outcomes. I was pursuing my PhD at NYU's School of Social Work where Phil was on the faculty running a course on executive nonprofit leadership. I wasted no time in signing up and enjoyed his witty style and stories of real challenges that I could relate to. I appreciated his wisdom, which emerged from his years of experience and although he was a highly regarded and influential CEO, he never forgot that he was a social worker. I admired how he connected his teaching to our profession's values of equity and social justice and made it a point to give everyone a voice. I thought about things I had learned from him and various mentors at CAS and how I carried those into my own leadership practice. These lessons, I came to see later on, were timeless; they transcended trends in "leadership style" and spoke to the realities executives encounter every day.

For example, I established All Staff Meetings at Inwood House where the entire agency could gather a few times a year. This gave staff members the opportunity to experience the agency as a whole and see how their area of work fit into the larger mission and structure. It also reflected a lesson Phil taught me, which is that contributions need to be invited. By building community within the agency, we were able to carry it out into the communities, schools, residences, and foster homes in which we operated. I found it amazing to reconnect with someone who had known me as a 22 year old and now as someone walking in similar footsteps to his. Little did we know in 2007 that there would be more of that.

In 2015, I had the opportunity to fulfill another dream in my career by joining the full-time faculty of NYU's Silver School of Social Work and assuming the role that Phil had inaugurated eight years prior as the Katherine & Howard Aibel Executive in Residence. We began to work together, recognizing that we were somewhat rare birds in academia with our experiences as CEOs. We shared a commitment to bring the macro practice perspective into classrooms filled with emerging social work professionals. Out of our conversations as colleagues at NYU Silver and our special history, the foundations for this book emerged. We were delighted, but not surprised, to find such alignment in our love for the social work profession, the field of human services, and our determination to see the profession fulfill its promise. We also shared concerns and caution at changes that we worried were rendering the profession less impactful precisely as social challenges demanded that we serve as true change agents. With almost 85 years of combined experience in the field we began this labor of love and urgency to engage our dear colleagues in the field in a "gut-check," a reflection in a time where we are experiencing not one, but multiple inflection points. The values, principles, and practices of our democracy are endangered while people suffer as much or more than at other times. Social work, as a profession anchored in values of social justice, self-determination, the dignity and worth of each individual, competency, and integrity has much to bring to the table of ideas, strategies, and knowledge for ameliorating human suffering and supporting the development of human potential. We must engage in leadership, appreciating the urgency during this period in history, mobilizing our fellow citizens to tackle the hard work of the change that is needed. This can only be done in partnership with others, like Phil, who recognize that this work is not just a profession, but a calling.

PHIL

Over 30 years ago I met Linda as a young social worker employed in CAS' Brooklyn office, which served status offenders referred by the Family Court. I recall on one of my visits the program director told me about a new young worker who was a wonderful addition to the staff and who had already established relationships with parents and teens from difficult family environments. The program was a special outreach to provide service to these youngsters who otherwise would face juvenile detention. It was not easy for staff to outreach, provide the needed help, develop a trusting relationship with both teens and their parents, and maintain ongoing connection to court personnel. Linda, I was told, fit the bill and even though new to the profession was the kind of staff member needed for such a delicate job. Over the next several years Linda grew in the position and her Director suggested to me that of her many staff members, Linda was the right person to present the program to our Board of Trustees. She did and made quite an impression on our Board and executive staff. Our Board left the meeting feeling not only well informed about the diversion program but also more aware of how difficult and demanding this work was.

Fast forward, Linda went on to get an MSW, worked as an executive in New York City's Administration for Children's Services, and over a period of years became the Executive Director of Inwood House, one of the most esteemed agencies in the city. While I had followed Linda's career, I was delighted when she both enrolled in my post-graduate seminar in Executive Leadership and subsequently, after completing her PhD, was selected by the NYU Silver School of Social Work as a member of the faculty.

Our new connection as colleagues was an experience in sharing our knowledge especially as it related to the training of social work leaders both in the Master's and the post-graduate programs. I was grateful that Linda, upon the recommendation of our Dean, would assume the Katherine and Howard Aibel Chair in Executive Leadership, an honor that I had previously enjoyed for 10 years. Hence began our collaboration, the result of which is this book which we hope will find an open mind in our profession and in the social service industry. It is indeed a time for change.

Introduction

In 2006, The J.P. Morgan Chase Foundation, The Children's Aid Society and The NYU Silver School of Social Work at NYU co-published a book by Philip Coltoff entitled *The Challenge of Change - Leadership Strategies for Not-for-profit Executives and Boards*. This book, uniquely readable and under 200 pages, was received quite well by the nonprofit world, especially in the field of social work. Over 25,000 copies were either sold or distributed to nonprofits supported by the J.P. Morgan Chase Foundation. All proceeds were contributed to the College Scholarship Fund established by The Children's Aid Society.

The book was one of the first directed to the nonprofit world featuring leadership strategies and practices. While Professor Linda Lausell Bryant of the NYU Silver School of Social Work and I began the process of writing and revising a new edition, we recognized that indeed a new book was called for. Too much has changed since 2006. While some of the strategies are still relevant, and are incorporated in this new book, the world in which we live has undergone remarkable and systemic changes that require new strategies, new approaches, and a new analysis of what leaders in our industry need to know and do. Hence this new book will attempt to focus on the world of 2021, its impact on its citizens, particularly those most marginalized and vulnerable, and the responses needed by organizations and agencies that serve these populations. It will focus, as well, on the universities and schools of social work that prepare the workforce, and on the professionals and boards who run these organizations and need to understand how their mission and practices must reflect the community and the world in which we now live.

The Great Recession of 2008 affected every segment of our society. The poor became poorer and more marginalized, agencies became more budget-conscious and less aggressive, and schools of social work, in many instances were teaching students using curricula and approaches no longer current. Social services were being eroded. Women and girls, newly arrived immigrants and refugees, the LGBTQ community, and communities of color were facing unprecedented attacks. Our former center-right wing government began moving away from a caring humanistic approach and toward mass incarceration, including more recently keeping "kids in cages" at our border. These interim years also brought a new political awakening. The Kaiser Family Foundation 2018 survey indicated that 1 in 5 Americans has either marched in the street or attended political rallies since 2016.[1] What were and are people protesting? Almost every major social issue — gun control, attacks on women's rights, lack of racial equity, diminished health care services to millions, police brutality, and overt forms of nationalism and racism. Throughout our system and the social work world, particularly in universities, students and faculty have begun to actively think and talk about social justice, human rights, economic rights, diversity, inclusion, community building, and bridging the divisions within our society. Our students are talking about white privilege, political and gender identity, and socioeconomic status. They want change.

When one examines these issues, it is clear that they fall right in the mainstream of our social work profession. Throughout our history we have been committed to serving those most in need and to redressing the ills of our society. This is our new moment, a time to use our leadership and our unique position within the social fabric to re-energize our profession, to teach and practice what's needed in today's world, and to move forward. This is what we hope to accomplish in this new book.

To assure a comprehensive approach, we have also reached out to key professional leaders across our networks to incorporate their thinking on what is required today. Such will be reflected in this edition.

Linda Lausell Bryant
Philip Coltoff

TABLE OF CONTENTS

PART I
SOCIAL WORK IN AN ERA
OF DEMOCRATIC EROSION

CHAPTER 1

PART III
EDUCATION AND PRACTICE

CHAPTER 6

PART IV
REFLECTIONS FROM SOCIAL
WORK EXECUTIVES

PART I
SOCIAL WORK
IN AN ERA
OF DEMOCRATIC
EROSION

CHAPTER 1

SOCIAL WORK AGENCIES: HISTORICAL CONTEXT, PRESENT CONSTRAINTS, AND POSSIBILITIES FOR THE FUTURE

Historical Context

The profession of social work has its roots in working with the poorest immigrant populations in the late 19th and 20th centuries. The settlement house movement, which began in the 1880s, started with University Settlement in New York City (1886) and Hull House in Chicago (1889). They initiated the first outreach programs to newly arrived immigrant populations. Large numbers of Irish, Italian, Eastern European, and European Jews arrived in the United States for both better economic opportunities and to avoid political persecution. Many programs evolved to serve these populations, largely under the aegis of the emerging social work profession. Community-based health and dental clinics, summer camps, "Friendly Visitors," and youth work programs all emerged during this period and constituted the core of social work intervention. At that time, all of these programs were voluntary in nature and supported by private contributions, largely from wealthy individuals. While many programs to help those experiencing poverty, or who were destitute or oppressed, continued to develop into the early and mid-twentieth century, government intervention in any substantial way did not emerge until the mid-1930s under the New Deal programs of President Franklin Delano Roosevelt.

Social work then grew and developed, and, under the influence of Freudian psychology, the profession began to address many of the emotional and psychological issues affecting poor and middle class people. As the immigrant population assimilated into the larger society, in many instances the second and third generation no longer required concrete assistance. The social work profession focused more on the behavioral and clinical issues of these populations. While social work as a practice and an industry always continued to have components of social reform and community organization, the major activities slowly shifted toward the clinical rather than the reformist. In the late-20th to early-21st century, the largest growth in social works' ever enlarging professional activities centered on psychotherapy and various other clinical approaches to behavior change, such as Cognitive Behavioral Therapy, Dialectical Behavioral Therapy, and Eye Movement Desensitization and Reprocessing. The individual and family were the central focus of social work intervention with the outcomes being defined as positive changes of behavior rather than changing the inequities of our society that helped produce dysfunctional behavior and social disorganization.

Present Constraints

Today our society is again facing a major demographic shift with substantial immigrant populations very much like the early days of the 20th century. The newly arrived populations are no longer European but rather come from Asia, Africa, and Latin America. The profession of social work is only starting to shift its orientation, after almost 100 years, toward recognizing once again the need for specific programs to help a newly arrived population. Not only is there a need for basic health, education, housing, and community services but a larger need to help these populations adjust to their new environment. In addition, our society must make changes to accept these new populations and to reduce the animosity and fear that often accompanies significant demographic shifts. Our profession must not only play a significant role but must play a leading role. Social work must not only restructure and redirect its services toward serving the poor directly through community centers, schools, and health clinics but also must work together with poor and immigrant communities to address larger social constraints and inequities.

The need for social work to re-orient toward macro issues was heightened by two major events: the 2008 Great Recession and the election of Donald Trump in 2016. These events required the profession as a whole to re-evaluate its mission, values, and purpose in this new climate.

The Great Recession of 2008

Few events have changed the nonprofit social services sector more than the Great Recession of 2008. With foundation endowments dropping precipitously in the immediate wake of the stock market crash, many of these institutions stopped issuing grants or greatly reduced them.[2] Many nonprofit boards were destabilized as corporate managers, a large number of whom are represented on many boards, were consumed with changes in their own workplaces, holding onto or losing their jobs due to the downsizing or closing of companies that followed the crash. There's a saying that "when Wall Street catches a cold, the nonprofit social services sector gets pneumonia." This economic decline impacted all social services for years, and arguably continues through the present.

The social services nonprofit sector has always had a symbiotic relationship with Wall Street and with corporate America. It depends on corporate America for trustees, funding, volunteers, and all forms of in-kind support. In symbiotic relationships, partners can adopt the values, perspectives, and strategies of one another. These things happen organically, often imperceptibly, and it helps to do a "gut-check" to make sure that our identity and values as a social services sector are still strongly aligned with the values and perspectives that should drive the work. A "gut-check" helps us to examine the ways in which market forces are impinging upon our work because we operate within and are subject to them. How can we adapt to these forces to stay competitive and stay in business without straying from or losing our core values? We imagine that few people would have any objection to the core values of social work, which on their face, do not seem to be threatening in any way. Strategically and tactically, however, embodying these values in our work will create a dynamic tension in the symbiotic relationship. The pursuit of social justice may require challenging our partners, our allies, and even the marketplace.

In our combined 85 years of experience in the field of social services, rarely has a funder explicitly required justice or equity as an outcome, but whether our required outcomes are to reduce foster care placement or to increase high school graduation rates, we know that these are inextricably linked to social justice. The difference between the expressed values of the social service nonprofit sector and the necessity for funds from government and corporate America is an inherent tension and likely to be so for the foreseeable future. How we navigate this tension has enormous implications for the children, youth, families, and individuals the sector serves.

The 2016 Election of Donald Trump

The election of Donald Trump in 2016 amplified the call to address social inequities and redirect social discourse. Under his administration, racial equity, gender equality, reproductive rights, immigration and immigrant rights, and individual liberties were under assault. Further, the stated policy of the 45th President, his administration, and in most instances the Congress – to belittle individuals who disagreed with him, cast honesty aside, and disparage and degrade minorities – required a strong organizational response.

The election led to the re-emergence of anti-democratic forces, white nationalism, anti-Semitism, and bigotry directed toward women and girls, minoritized youth, and the LGBTQ community. Many of these developments had been festering for years and had been hidden but ever present as part of the American experience. While these expressions had remained largely latent, they were unleashed by the then Presidential hierarchy, particularly at the national level. Our communities were affected by the misogyny, fear, anxiety and economic despair that accompanies such open and destructive activities directed toward people who are seen as different, and a threat.

Social work has historically always been at the forefront on issues that affect the populations that often make up our constituents. A recent article in the JAMA Internal Medicine journal found that opioid deaths were 85% higher in counties where automotive plants had closed.[3] This is only one example of how economic despair affects public health, a correlation that research has substantiated.[4] One cannot ignore the intense social and psychological effects on people during times of great economic stress. Similarly, behavioral and psychological issues of self-doubt, lower self-esteem, and at times suicidal thoughts are causal and conditional consequences of economic dysfunction. Social workers are often required in both our agencies and even in private practice to deal with these behavioral issues.

The Anti-Defamation League released a report indicating that between 2018 and 2019, there was a 12% increase in antisemitic incidents, with a 56% increase in antisemitic assaults.[5] Antisemitism's durability to reinvent itself should never be underestimated. This is just one example of how our current political climate affects our populace and can unleash destructive vestiges of the past. A 2019 article by Bernard P. Dreyer in the New England Journal of Medicine discusses the "state of siege" that Latino children and families are experiencing due to harsh immigration policies and the impact this has on their health and mental health.[6]

Recently there have been scores of articles on the state of our environment and the effects of climate change. Some in elected positions have been disrespectful and sarcastic about Greta Thunberg, a now 17 year old, who has taken on this issue and become a worldwide leader, attempting to alert all of us to the devastating effects of burning fossil fuels. Thunberg's views are closer to the consensus of noted scientists and economists than those of our former President and his administration, and yet she is mocked.

The election of Joe Biden to the Presidency was indeed good news and reflects more the goals and purposes of the social work profession. We must also recognize the enormous numbers of voters who reflected a dysfunctional if not racist and xenophobic view of America. If anything, these events indicate we must be even more vigilant in our efforts to combat injustice, racism, and inequality in all spheres of life. Schools of social work, and our profession in general, need to find our place in the center of both the resistance and the movement toward social change.

The social work profession, with others, needs to protect and defend vulnerable communities from the erosion of constitutional liberties. Organizations must develop advocacy programs that resist this form of dehumanization and continue to offer the public a sense of hope, promise, and fulfillment. Democracy for the social work profession is not an abstract concept but a living dynamic that continually needs strengthening and support. In fact, social work cannot truly function in any system other than a democracy.

Future Possibilities: Social Workers as Change Agents

Social work is at a crossroads. Its work has never been more essential and yet the profession has focused on direct service provision and unintentionally minimized advocacy and social action. Over the past two decades, a tension has developed over the profession's role, values, and purpose in an increasingly constrained social service environment. Those who occupy leadership roles – in agencies, nonprofits, and universities – have an important role to make this tension generative and recommit to social work's core mission

At one time, community based social service agencies – settlements, neighborhood houses, YM-YWCA and YM-YWCHAs, the Girl Scouts of America, and faith-based organizations – welcomed young people and provided settings in which they could explore and express their thoughts on issues such as civil rights, preventing war, civil liberties, world peace, nuclear disarmament, and many other issues. Today, one would have to look hard and long to find social work-directed youth services with similar programming. Many of our agencies have taken the safe road. One finds young people playing basketball, doing crafts, having dance lessons – all of which is fine, but agencies should also offer opportunities to discuss the major national dilemmas, problems, fears, and promises that exist in all communities throughout our nation. If we do not provide such opportunities for our youth, young people will find other options that offer less democratic and humanistic experiences.

Some in our profession will say that what we are presently offering are also extremely valuable services and indeed they may be right. We are not suggesting that all of the services and activities that we are currently providing should be disregarded or are of a retrograde nature. Rather, we are suggesting that a careful analysis should be made across the social work profession and by each organization of their activities and missions so that we can expand what we are doing in ways that will be more relevant to the social, cultural, and psychological issues of the day. We are not suggesting mission creep; we are suggesting mission relevance and impact.

At the time of this writing, during a turbulent time of crisis throughout the nation, social service leaders at the local and national level need to project a sense of hopefulness, openness, and opportunity to their communities and constituents. Many communities, particularly minoritized communities, feel a sense of disengagement and, in many instances, fear and oppression. Our former senior political figures provoked feelings of not being welcomed or wanted. It is precisely because of this that nonprofits must maintain a sense of hope, safety, and commitment to equality and the basic values of democracy. When people feel disregarded, disdained, and depressed there is almost always a reaction of both fear and self-protection. It is especially during these challenging times that agency advocacy and engagement are among the most important qualities of social work leadership.

This is the time for social workers and our formal organizations to step forward to confront those ideas which threaten our democratic way of life. At a time when the wealthiest one percent of households own 40% of the U.S.'s wealth, social work can provide us with guideposts to correct this imbalance.[7] It was our professional forbearers that led the way to social reform and political change in the areas of housing, education, suffrage, immigrant rights, and community activism. The extent to which social service agencies understand and embrace their role as social reformers will determine the impact and effectiveness of our leadership.

With changing times, there are also strong political overtones to issues that were once within the professional arena, such as the Black Lives Matter movement, incarceration among Black, Indigenous, and other People of Color (BIPOC) youth, LGBTQ rights, and the #MeToo movement, to name a few. Our role is to help empower a new generation of social workers to lead the change, emerge as leaders, and understand the functions of advocacy and activism. Agencies need to move away from "putting out fires" and begin to address the long-term and more fundamental needs of their clients. Our agencies must stand boldly for the rights of poor, minoritized, and marginalized people in much the way that our professional forebearers stood squarely for serving "the halt, the lame, and the deserving poor." We must create a new social compact that redresses the evident inequities and apparent ills of the social system.

Chapter 1 Questions
For Students:

1. How has the history of social work informed your understanding of the role and function of our profession today?

2. In your view, have we as a profession marginalized our reformist tradition to achieve a professional status within the behavioral sciences?

For Educators and Academic Administrators:

1. Have the restraints of university policy limited your ability to adequately advocate for social change?

2. How can Deans and other academic leaders prioritize macro- and policy-oriented education and training for students?

Reader's Notes:

AGENCIES AS ACTIVISTS: SOCIAL WORK'S RESPONSE TO THE PANDEMIC AND THE MOVEMENT FOR RACIAL JUSTICE

We live in politically volatile times. Many nonprofits have continued to operate on reduced or sometimes austere budgets since the Great Recession. This has hampered their advocacy efforts, as many allocate their resources exclusively toward direct service provision. While many of today's social service organizations can seem risk-averse when it comes to advocacy, historically speaking, social work has been at the forefront of social justice movements.

An Activist Approach in Social Work

Social workers and social service agencies must reassess and reevaluate their mission, purpose, and programmatic activities in the light of the changes in our social system and the imperatives to address social, cultural, and behavioral issues. The social work profession's roots are grounded in 19th century social movements that aimed to address the economic and social problems affecting poor, disenfranchised, and largely immigrant populations. One can examine the scope of these social work activities in the work of Jane Adams and the Chicago-based Hull House, the emergence of the Settlement House Movement in New York, the activities of organizations such as The Children's Aid Society, City Mission Society, Community Service Society, and the early movements such as the Society for Improving the Conditions of the Poor, Little Orphans Society, and the Foundlings' Orphan Train phenomenon.

Many social service agencies, while being direct service providers, have also engaged in larger community issues or public advocacy. This role sometimes referred to as "external relations" was a major function of social work in the 1930s, where the profession played a major role in the development of the social safety net. Building on the accomplishments of the 1930s and 1960s, The Children's Aid Society developed a working formula that was very helpful in the integration of our direct service and community advocacy. This approach was referred to as "SERVICE PLUS ADVOCACY EQUALS CHANGE." The advent of McCarthyism in the 1950s constrained social work advocacy for fear of community or governmental reprisal. Many social service agencies chose to look inward and concentrate on service provision, fearing exposure with negative effect if they actively engaged in social change. While the 1960s reintroduced activism, its effect was not long lasting. Advocacy was always secondary or tertiary at best. Many social work executives and boards hid behind their antiquated mission statements which limited their influence both in the community and in public discourse. Social work no longer served its major function of being "a gadfly on the social conscious." And yet, an activist approach is central to re-imagining how social work can respond to the two most pressing issues of our time: the pandemic and the movement for racial justice.

Social Work's Response to the Pandemic

Over the years, the social work profession has been responsive when disasters, major economic downturns, and health crises have occurred. The most recent example of social work's responsive role took place after September 11th and Hurricanes Katrina, Sandy, and Maria. After 9/11, many social service agencies, particularly in the New York area, were first responders providing emergency relief, housing, and health services. Following the immediate crisis many social service agencies, in partnership with government, trade unions and religious institutions, provided in-school and after school programs, scholarships for children left dependent by the death of a family member, and both job counseling and placement for displaced workers. These actions were not short lived and garnered considerable recognition from the general community, the media, and the philanthropic world. The most responsive agencies received funding for the unique programs they offered that went beyond their traditional mission and enabled them to truly be recognized along with the police, fire department, EMS, and government as first responders.

The COVID-19 pandemic also saw many social service agencies enter the arena by providing assistance. Most of these organizations were those that were community-based and in some measure viewed themselves as providing community direction and stability. The community trusted their work and turned to them for services, support, and reassurance, even though pandemic relief is not explicitly in their mandate. Many provided extensive programs which were not budgeted for such as homecare, after school programs, and mental health intervention for children and in some cases the entire family. They also delivered full meals to families that were shut in and paid emergency leave for staff who were not able to perform due to their own compromised health.

Several settlement houses, Catholic Charities of New York and Brooklyn Dioceses, enlarged their residential programs for those requiring immediate housing or quarantine while others provided free transportation to and from health facilities. These and other emergency programs were in keeping with the social work tradition of responding to crisis and community need.[8]

Unlike the 9/11 or hurricane aftermaths, additional funding from public or private sources was not forthcoming. Because of the total lock down and the immediate loss of jobs and revenues to both municipal government as well as the funding world, most first responder agencies raided their rainy day funds, tapped into their endowments, or in many instances borrowed so they could continue their vital services. There is a need for new funding streams to ensure that these organizations can not only continue to provide these vital services but in some cases survive. Either the government needs to come to the rescue or the formation of a partnership of major foundations must step into the funding role, as they have done in the past, to sustain operations. The leadership for this significant undertaking could come from municipal community trusts, religious federations, and prominent philanthropists.

Many other agencies, however, were unprepared to deal with the COVID-19 crisis. While some organizations, such as those that operate in hospitals, nursing homes, and congregate care facilities for children and adults, were deemed "essential" many were not and followed the general instruction to shelter-in-place. As a result, they were unable to continue service to their clients. These organizations, such as settlement houses and community centers, as well as those of a clinical nature, could not provide needed services to their clients suffering from severe anxiety or depression or in some cases Post Traumatic Stress Disorder.

Some, after a period of reflection, did provide online therapy or offered safe walk-in emergency services. Others considered opening their camps and residential facilities in a safe way for family use thus creating socialization programs and reducing the tensions arising from continuous family contact. The same is true with outreach provided to treat domestic violence and alcohol and drug abuse that accelerated during the crisis. These functions were left to the police which, most now recognize, could have been better provided by social workers.

Clearly, few if any were prepared to face this emergent crisis which in some parts of the country led to employment, educational, and economic lockdowns. Each agency learning from this experience should have a plan in place for how to respond to these emergencies. Many agencies have developed a "crisis management plan" with appropriate responses to situations arising in the community that affect the agency and its clients. A similar plan now needs to be developed to effectively respond to health emergencies such as a pandemic.

If all social agencies had a crisis management plan in place, they could have responded more immediately and appropriately. These programs could have been of a digital nature or, with safety precautions, in house. Most organizations would welcome an opportunity for professional staff and boards of directors to carefully examine their roles and functions since it certainly appears that COVID-19 will not be an isolated event. Climate change, political disorder, and community change will be upon us and require a response.

Community organizations, schools of social work, and at a larger scale, our professional associations need to advance a clear agenda for social change. The pandemic has been a threat of epochal proportions to low-income children. Poverty is causal to many of the poor outcomes in health and education but money and the resources that it provides can redress many of these issues. Countries facing the pandemic such as Canada, the UK, and many other European countries provide a systematic built-in children's allowance. With these funds, families were able to cope better, hire tutors, access health facilities, and most importantly avoid hunger. Our profession should advance a national program of children's allowances to both poor and middle class families. The high level of child poverty in the U.S.

demands such a response. Our national advocates must assure adequate reimbursement and new funding for localities earmarked for children and family interventions. While poverty has many aspects and causes, money will buy food, housing, and in some cases better schools. It reduces stress on parents thus enabling them to more effectively parent their children.

There is no age group for whom the pandemic does not pose a threat. Studies have shown a sharp increase in child hunger, witnessing the long lines for food distribution. We also need to more strenuously advance and enlarge the food stamp and subsidized breakfast and lunch programs in public schools. While one argument against a child allowance is the cost of roughly $100 billion a year, it is still less than one half of Donald Trump's tax cuts that mostly benefited the wealthy.

A National Policy for Emergency Response

How should our professional organizations, such as the National Association of Social Workers, the Council on Social Work Education, and the National Social Welfare Assembly develop national policy positions needed to align themselves for positive change? When national policy is advanced it becomes a non-binding guidepost on member agencies within the professional orbit. Policies that address the first responder role for social work would be most helpful to boards of directors and professional staff to address new areas of work which may not have previously fit neatly into the mission statement of a given agency. Too many agencies rest on their narrow mission statements which in most cases do not speak to large community crises such as pandemics, social disorder, or even social justice issues. Agency missions should always be subject to review and change based upon demographics, economics, and social needs. However, organizational change occurs too slowly. If our national organizations had clearly articulated and developed a policy direction it would facilitate local agencies and institutions to move beyond their present service parameters and see themselves as part of first responder infrastructure.

This shift in mindset is essential because it allows the entire professional community, from boards of directors to executives, to raise and set aside emergency funding. There is an unspoken assumption that agencies will carry out operations on a shoestring budget and even expand services to assist clients in economically challenging times. Yet, as more agencies close their doors in the midst of the pandemic, it's evident that this assumption is not only financially untenable but harmful. We, as a professional community, would be less paralyzed and more ready to face these new challenges if each agency had a crisis fund or endowment. Boards of directors, with proper education, would also be more responsive to the changing mission, provide the necessary dollars, and where necessary release reserve or endowment funds to support these new directions. Additionally, agencies can operate as a collective to bid for service contracts or proactively reach out to funders. One example is after 9/11, when many agencies that became known as first responders raised double or triple annual donations because their services were recognized as vital. Public perception of what we do is central to social work carrying out its crucial functions.

Social Work's Role in The Racial Justice Movement

The pandemic however, as a factor that upended our social realities, was somewhat eclipsed by a sustained demand for justice and equity embodied in movements and catalyzed by high-profile episodes of police brutality resulting in the deaths of Black individuals. Social work, like any other profession, has not been immune to the legacy and omnipresent bitter fruits of systemic racism. This is something that we, as a profession, have always needed to, and still need to, reckon with. This has been done across the human services sector to widely varying degrees, from no reckoning to some. While there is no facet of American life that is untouched by systemic racism, the social work profession with its espoused values of social justice, integrity, the dignity and worth of each individual, and its role in assisting individuals, families, and communities to recover from the effects of systemic racism, must hold itself to a higher level of accountability and work hard to ensure that we are actively working to be anti-racist, rather than less racist. Furthermore, recovery from the impacts of systemic racism and injustice is necessary but not sufficient. The very systems that perpetuate these injustices must be challenged, consistently, relentlessly, and as a matter of mission. While the social work profession has throughout its history been clearly on the side of democratic reform, equal opportunity, and self-determination, recent events have highlighted these issues in stark terms requiring our profession to re-examine both our values and the action implementation which derives from them. To accomplish these immediate and necessary tasks at both national and local levels we must institute the following steps:

1. *Develop a true partnership with activist organizations within BIPOC communities. In this partnership, social service agencies must leverage their capacity to secure funding and charitable donations to implement activities.*

2. *Police reform as a matter of course needs to be supported and activated. A sustained dialogue with affected communities about the history and nature of policing is long overdue. We need a zero tolerance policy for choke holds and other life threatening restraints and we must position ourselves to advocate for accountability, including punishment for police brutality and corruption. Specifically, within the reform package social workers, particularly those trained in community organization and*

group work, can be a part of the "refunding" of police departments throughout the country.

The social work profession does not have a consensus on how to approach the issue of its role vis-a-vis police departments and the criminal legal system. New York University faculty, students and others signed on to a call for social workers, including student interns, to not work or be placed within these institutions. This goes to a foundational debate about how best to bring about change – whether from within or from outside. We suggest that the magnitude of tackling systemic racism and injustice requires activism from within and without but here again, we need to create spaces for sustained dialogue and exploration about our role in these contexts. Social workers are better equipped to deal with domestic violence, youth delinquency, truancy, school suspensions, and other juvenile justice issues than are the police. When such reform occurs, social workers, unlike their predecessors who were part of the Society for the Prevention of Cruelty to Children, will carry appropriate identification but not a weapon.

3. *Social work in many cases has been part of public school reform, such as within community schools or charter schools. These efforts should be intensified, and we should provide such services in alliance with Black, Latino and other minoritized communities, who are least well-served by public schools that reflect segregation in resources and in educational outcomes. Teachers, social workers, and healthcare providers will be part of this initiative with recruiting efforts directed toward historically Black colleges and universities.*

4. *Racism is embedded and often revolves around the economy. Our economic system currently reflects two distinct Americas, one white and one non-white. Our profession must intensify efforts to recruit students of color into our Bachelor, Masters, and Doctorate programs. Adequate provision for scholarship assistance needs to be part of the recruitment. Our profession aims to serve poor communities, which are disproportionately non-white. It should not be served by a profession which currently remains almost 70% white.[9] Universities that house and support schools of social work should be lobbied to understand the*

unique role of social work in today's America and release a portion of their endowment funds and reserves to this recruiting and scholarship activity. We understand that there are many demands for university scholarship assistance and that the amount of funds available for such assistance varies depending on the size of the endowment. At the policy level we should actively support "fair employment practices," a living wage for all workers (at the present time, $20.00 per hour), as well as government or employer paid health insurance, sick leave, and childcare benefits. Advancing these policies will align our profession with progressive Black, Latino, LGBTQ, and trade union movements.

5. *Environmental justice is a central concern of all communities but, once again, racial disparities are most evident. Toxic environments, and not just in Flint, Michigan but throughout our country, are mostly found in non-white communities. These environmental issues lead to extreme childhood asthma, blood toxicity, and in some cases premature death.*

6. *While social work has always been at the forefront of the provision of health and mental health services for poor communities, we must accelerate this activity at both the practice and policy levels. We should finally advance the concept of Medicare For All. Only with such an umbrella service, delivered at the local level, will there ever be assured access to quality and affordable health and mental health care.*

7. *Social work service providers, especially community-based agencies, should reintroduce outreach programs such as voter registration campaigns that include transportation for voters to get to the polls. They should also offer open town hall meetings on a consistent basis to listen to community residents, including youth, and not just consumers of services. Through these meetings they will hear concerns and have the opportunity to develop partnerships and establish activist remedies.*

It is essential for the social work profession to amplify the voices of affected communities and demand sustained action and change. We need to partner with communities, sharing the tools we have such as knowledge of how systems work. There has been some collective gnashing of teeth around the lack of basic civics education in the nation's public education curriculum and while that gap is real, as a profession, our engagement in social action can and should include demystifying the workings of our government systems. This would allow communities to most effectively target the appropriate levers to advocate for change. As a profession, our goal should remain one of partnership with communities to achieve the changes they seek and that cannot be achieved through individually focused casework. Here, we need to turn to community organizing and group work processes that can build on the collective strength, wisdom, intelligence, and aspirations of the communities we aim to help.

At NYU Silver, we have been engaged in efforts to "walk our talk."[10] We have reacted to the voices of students and are working to be more proactive and thorough in our efforts. The curriculum has been revised so that it is anchored in social justice, standpoint theory, anti-oppressive practice, intersectionality and critical race theory. Recognizing that the classroom is not the only locus of change, NYU Silver has hired an inaugural Director of Diversity, Equity, and

Inclusion and has more robustly operationalized its Social Justice Praxis Committee, which is composed of faculty, staff, and students. In order to strengthen antiracist pedagogy, we have convened a pedagogy support workgroup, co-chaired by faculty members Linda Lausell Bryant and Doris Chang. This led to the implementation of a semester-long, comprehensive faculty anti-racism training for all full and part-time faculty. Additionally, Drs. Lausell Bryant and Chang launched a Peer Consultation Program in which faculty with expertise in anti-racism pedagogy can coach and consult with others to augment our collective capacity to conduct classes that are inclusive, attuned to issues of diversity, and promote anti-oppressive practice. We have also partnered with NYU's Office of Global Inclusion, spearheaded by our first Chief Diversity Officer, Lisa Coleman. Like so many institutions of higher education we have work to do to address systemic racism within our own organization while educating students to do the same. Higher education is not nearly as diverse, inclusive, or equitable as it could be or needs to be to best serve an increasingly diverse student population. We have and continue to advocate for and engage in initiatives that support NYU's acknowledgment of the work it needs to do as an institution, while educating students to become the kinds of citizens that value and practice justice, equity and inclusion. From our perspective, an activist approach begins with honest reflection of our own shortcomings, our own contributions to the problems, be it by commission or omission, so that we can engage in change from a place of awareness and commit to it in deeds and not just words.

As a society, organizations have begun to recognize that it is not good business to ignore these issues. Frequently, the response has been to "appear" to be activist by issuing statements in support of diversity, equity and inclusion, or to give lip service to such values without committing to the work of transformation, which calls for sustained, ongoing work. It is incumbent upon our profession to call for, coax, coach, demand and hold accountable organizations that provide human services but that fail to fully respect the humanity of those they serve.

Our profession is truly at a crossroads, as are many other professions, and we should seize upon these crises to move social work forward in ways that have a positive impact on changing our society to become a more fair and equal union.

Chapter 2 Questions
For Students:

1. What does it mean to take an anti-racist approach in social work practice? What would you like to see added to the social work curriculum to help equip you to practice in an anti-racist and anti-oppressive manner?

2. What observations and lessons have emerged from your field placement organization's response to the pandemic? How have your field placements responded to the movement for racial justice?

For Educators and Academic Administrators:

1. Is it possible or practical to hold true to social work values in the face of a funding crisis?

2. Political considerations aside, have we sufficiently centered the issues of racism, sexism, ageism, and anti-Semitism in policy and practice?

Reader's Notes:

PART II
A NEW LEADERSHIP PARADIGM

CHAPTER 3
ADAPTIVE LEADERSHIP

Re-imagining Leadership in the Human Services Context

There is no shortage of leadership models with accompanying books, articles, videos and courses. In these many theories, models and frameworks, leadership tends to be defined in many ways and however it is defined, there is strong consensus on the importance of leadership on organizational effectiveness. Less developed are the theories and research on the alignment between leadership frameworks and specific professional contexts or situations. What leadership theories or frameworks make sense for the social work profession and the human services context? Leadership has not received the emphasis it requires within the social work profession, surely for many reasons, some anchored in our professional identities as helpers who are not focused on hierarchies or power. We believe that the profession's under-emphasis on leadership as a core element of social work has dimmed the impact that we can and should have on the major social challenges that we face.

Many theories approach the issue of leadership by emphasizing the centrality of the person considered the "leader," especially their traits and behaviors and how they influence the organization. Other leadership theories focus on the factors that facilitate the emergence of leadership and some emphasize the context or situation and the interaction of all of these components. The "metrics" of leadership vary wildly, from organizational budget size and growth to media presence to charisma. We consider it essential that organizations examine their explicit and implicit leadership frameworks and how well they are aligned to the purpose of the organization and the impact it aims to bring about. In keeping with social work performing a "gut-check" on ourselves, we need to ask ourselves "What is it that we believe about the purpose and function of leadership, about who is equipped to exercise leadership, and about whether leadership is learned or intrinsic?"

What are the implications of being grounded in values such as social justice while being symbiotically tied to other sectors that may prioritize other values? How can we operate effectively within these multiple arenas while advancing our missions? How can we ensure that in carrying out our work, we are not perpetuating the very injustices and inequities we profess to be fighting?

Our leadership models and approaches should reflect our purposes. Broadly speaking, social work's purpose is to alleviate human suffering and strengthen human potential and social functioning by focusing on the relationship between the person and his/her/their environment. When we put this purpose into the current context, we believe that these times call for a doubling down on the values of the social work profession such as social justice, a value for the dignity and worth of each individual, and a focus on integrity and competence. As we reflect upon our experience in the human services sector, we can appreciate how much time and effort we've had to focus on ensuring that our agencies could survive, and at times, thrive, in a challenging, competitive, and under-resourced market. And while there is no doubt that these efforts allowed our agencies to provide services that helped countless children, youth and families, was it enough? Is it enough to feed the hungry and clothe the naked? It is indeed necessary, but is it sufficient? We propose that we need to challenge the very social structures that allow poverty, homelessness, and a host of social problems to be normative, including a human services sector that can help some without totally upending such a status quo. Can we work within this structure and shake it up? Challenge it? Can we bring justice while working within an unjust set of systems? We must. We propose that if our purpose in the sector is to create the kind of change that will bring us closer to justice for all, to valuing the dignity and worth of each individual, then our leadership models need to be commensurate with that purpose.

Managing a nonprofit human service agency is incredibly complicated and requires a wide array of skills, competencies, and technical knowledge. It has probably always been the case but in our view, it seems that it is increasingly complex, perhaps due to more competition for scarce resources as the number of nonprofits has grown. Sociopolitical shifts have influenced the tone and tenor of ongoing debates about national priorities. The country has had two presidents in the past decade who differ from the historical, traditional mold. We have had our first African-American president and our first president with no government experience. Both presidencies have surfaced deeply rooted perspectives on the nature of leadership and who should be deemed a "leader." Deeply rooted perspectives on race and race in relationship to authority have also surfaced. We continue to engage in the perennial debate about poverty and who is worthy of human services and what the root causes are when some people aren't self-sufficient. The debate also includes whose responsibility it is to provide help. Government? The private sector? Is poverty a reflection of personal failing or the result of systemic inequality? There's been increased regulation of the sector given the government resources it receives. There is increased pressure to show evidence of one's impact and a multiplying amount of accountability documentation. The sector is evaluated based on how much it can do with the least amount of resources. One of the impacts of the increasing complexity of the sector is the work it takes to manage it, respond to it, adapt to it, and feed the beast. Little time and energy and other resources are left to question it, let alone change it. Our approaches to change are increasingly modeled on the corporate world and focused on survival of the fittest. But are we having the impact we seek? Are we helping to bring about the change we seek that is encapsulated in our missions? That our clients are seeking?

Managing a human services agency requires humility, a recognition that however skillful, talented and competent one might be, it is highly likely that none of us has all of the answers to the complex social challenges faced by the constituents we serve. Of course, in our current times, when social perspectives are increasingly commodified, humility may be seen as just another competency to be showcased. But what we refer to here is a genuine peace with not having all of the answers while trusting that solutions and innovations can be derived through the efforts, ideas, intelligence, experience, and wisdom of the collective organization and its key stakeholders.

Defining Adaptive Leadership

So, what is leadership in the human services context? We offer some thoughts here about how we think about leadership from a social work perspective and in the context of human services. Upon reflection of how we each previously came to understand leadership, we viewed it as a set of skills and competencies that resided within us, acquired through learning, both academic and experiential, that enabled us to have the wisdom to know how to set direction to the work and get people "on board" with our direction which was grounded in our social work-informed values. We built and cultivated relationships and made sure to not have people feel that they were being lorded over. We were humanistic in our approaches and we engaged in communications that framed the issues as we saw them and how our agencies embodied the answers or needed solutions. We did this well, and we even worked to build new leaders from our teams, seeking those skills and competencies that we possessed and even some we did not, because we had good eyes for judging such talent. Clearly, this is an oversimplified synopsis of many leadership frameworks in which the person who plays the role of the organizational leader is presumed to possess leadership. Notice the centrality of the person who occupies the role of the "leader."

What if we think of leadership as neither skill or competency, as neither role nor position, but simply as something we do, an activity, perhaps an activity motivated by a purpose? This simple notion means that people can engage in leadership, can exercise leadership, from whatever roles they may occupy in organizations and in society. That would mean that leadership is the purview, privilege, and responsibility of many, perhaps even all, rather than the few who occupy positions of authority within an organization. This is a simple, yet radical idea that suggests that anyone can exercise leadership. It is not something that some people have, and others do not. This is one of the underpinnings of adaptive leadership, developed by Ronald Heifetz and Marty Linsky at the Harvard Kennedy School over 35 years ago.[11] This framework is the theoretical underpinning to the courses, training institute and initiatives at NYU Silver introduced by Dr. Lausell Bryant in partnership with her colleague, Marc Manashil, with the aim of strengthening the leadership capacities of social workers in training and other human services professionals (see Appendix A for learning objectives and outcomes). If leadership is not dependent on one's role or position, it means no one has to wait to have a title or role bestowed on them in order to take action. How does that feel? Liberating? Uncomfortable? Both?

The roles or positions that we hold as "leaders" may or may not be related to leadership as something we do. It is often more so reflective of possessing authority, which has been formally or informally bestowed upon us, and we maintain that authority as long as we fulfill the responsibilities that we have been asked to do and that we have agreed to do. We tend to refer to people in authority, such as the CEO, the director, the president, and Deans, as leaders. And our hope is that our "leaders" will exercise leadership. In fact, as many water coolers would attest if they could speak, many workers bemoan the fact that their leaders are not leading. This distinction between leadership and authority is crucial to understand in the adaptive leadership framework because it focuses on the function of each, and the proper application of each in the practice context. Authority, a concept that at times is fraught with negative associations, has an important function in society and organizations, which is to provide protection, direction and order. It is essential to a civil society.

In addition to the distinction between leadership and

authority, there is also a distinction in the types of challenges we face and how they relate to leadership and authority. Heifetz and Linsky distinguish between technical and adaptive challenges. Technical challenges are those that can be addressed by the application of knowledge. There is a known solution for them, borne out by knowledge or expertise and if this is applied, generally, a solution can be reached. These aren't necessarily simple challenges but if you can access the knowledge and expertise, you can likely resolve the challenge. If you are on a plane and the air filtration system is not working, someone with expertise can theoretically address that challenge. Adaptive challenges, on the other hand, are those that tend to be about "root" issues, the proverbial elephant in the room, such as differences in values and perspectives and to make progress on these types of challenges, it will not suffice to just apply knowledge or expertise. In fact, there is no one "leader" who can come up with THE solution to an adaptive challenge. The challenges we work to tackle within social work are primarily adaptive challenges with no easy or singular answers. Has anyone single handedly solved racism or injustice? Of course not, though progress has been made. Adaptive challenges have no easy answers or specific solutions and require innovation. The best road to innovative ideas lies in a multiplicity of perspectives, the collective intelligence. In many organizations, the adaptive challenge of racism in the workplace is often addressed in a technical manner with diversity or anti-racism workshops. This is not to say that these interventions are without merit or value. But in and of themselves, they cannot "solve" racism. They can be a tool in a larger strategy of addressing the complex web of values, perspectives, loyalties, policies, and practices that sustain organizational racism, but we cannot apply diversity workshops in the same manner as we would take two pain relievers when experiencing a headache. Our efforts at making progress on the adaptive challenges of our time are undermined and stymied when we fail to appreciate the deeply layered nature of these challenges and instead, treat them as technical challenges. There is no "one and done" or "magic bullet" to addressing adaptive challenges. And here is why leadership frameworks are so important and need to be aligned with the work. Importing leadership models from other industries or professions, especially corporate businesses, may fail to support the nature of social justice work.

The principal leadership framework is the adaptive leadership framework, which is now being advanced by a growing community of educators around the world. Its premise is that organizations and communities must be able to adapt to rapidly changing circumstances if they wish to thrive, and even survive. In this context, the work of leadership is about helping people figure out which practices to preserve, which ones to discard, and what new innovations can help them function more effectively in a changing environment.

Students of adaptive leadership initially work to better understand the stakeholder system of which they are a part, and specifically the values, loyalties, and potential losses that influence stakeholder actions in the face of change. The purpose of this "diagnostic" is to help practitioners better understand both the sources of support and resistance as they attempt to mobilize people in the direction of progress.[12] Heifetz describes leadership as mobilizing people to face the tough work they need to tackle in order to achieve progress. He describes leadership as "disappointing people at a rate that they can stand." Leadership as disappointment? How so? Well, to mobilize people is to disrupt the status quo, the state that is comfortable because it is familiar, even if it is miserable. Change is disruptive and people tend to resist change, even change we desperately want. Have you ever tried to lose weight? I (Linda) am expert in that struggle. This is a change that I want and I welcome. Facing the hard work to achieve it is far more complex than counting calories and sit-ups. I am motivated and I can just imagine how great it will be when I get there. In fact, that may even sustain my efforts for a short time. Most challenges have technical aspects as well as adaptive ones. Weight loss is not just a technical challenge for me (and probably many others as well). It is not just an issue of applying existing knowledge and expertise to lose weight, but it is also about deeper issues, ones which have no easy answers but involve tough work. I might have to examine cultural norms around body types, cultural values around women's bodies, issues of sexual trauma, childhood issues related to food and poverty, identity issues and even all that will change, including relationships, when the numbers on the scale change. So, while a larger weight may be uncomfortable, it is familiar and, in some ways, feels safer than the journey into the less familiar lesser weight.[13]

Adaptive Leadership in Organizational Practice: Implications for Human Services Organizations and Practice

So, what does this have to do with an organization? In the adaptive leadership framework, organizational systems resist change, not necessarily consciously, even as they pursue change consciously. Each member of the organization has their own values, loyalties to people and perspectives and stands to lose something if change happens. This is even when there is strong consensus that things need to change. And so, we struggle to make progress on key issues while dealing with the persistent resistance to change that comes from us and others in the system. Understanding and managing that resistance is a key part of leadership work.

While a thorough analysis of various leadership models is out of the scope of this book, our purpose here is to invite you to reflect upon the leadership frameworks, models and philosophies that guide your work in the human services context and to examine the alignment of the framework(s) with the purpose and mission you strive to achieve. Where are the tensions in practice? In our experience, a framework like adaptive leadership that is grounded in the idea that leadership can be exercised by anyone, regardless of role or position, is more conducive to practicing in ways that are inclusive and that recognize value coming from throughout the organization. Since the objective is change of the status quo, adaptive leadership is in essence, an activist orientation.

We also need social workers to assume roles of authority in the field as CEOs and senior managers. We have seen a trend in the last 30 years that the CEO ranks of human services agencies are less filled with social work-trained individuals. It is not our thesis that only social work-trained professionals should run human services agencies. Our thought, however, is that the sector isn't best served by social workers comprising the minority in senior management roles.

Ric Estrada, MSW, MBA has been the CEO of Metropolitan Family Services (MFS) in Chicago for almost a decade now. He began working at the agency as a social work intern and after years of experience in the field, returned to MFS as the CEO. MFS considers itself Chicago's legacy nonprofit and is considered among a handful of such organizations, founded in 1857, predating Hull House by

30 years. Jane Addams served on their board for 30 years as she worked on child welfare laws. Mr. Estrada says that MFS considers itself a true social work organization where a social work degree is needed to rise through the ranks. The CEO, COO, and Executive Director all hold MSWs. Mr. Estrada also pursued an MBA to bolster his credibility as someone who could manage, especially financially. In Ric's experience, social work credentialed individuals bring practice experience and a systems perspective with greater awareness of the many complex issues involved in the challenges the agency faces.

We are appreciative of Heifetz and Linsky's contributions of the adaptive leadership framework and their efforts to have it be applicable across a wide variety of settings, from nonprofit to corporate and beyond. Our contribution to this work is to enhance its application in the context of the human services arena and those who work in it, particularly social workers. We aim to strengthen its application to the adaptive challenge that is racism and its impact on diversity, equity and inclusion in the human services sector and beyond.

In practice, adaptive leaders must resist the temptation and the strong pull to provide answers for their teams. Instead, they can emphasize the engagement of the team, or system, in the process of confronting the challenges, understanding who the key stakeholders are, and learning what perspectives they hold with respect to the challenge. They need to help uncover or surface hidden perspectives. This flies in the face of everything we associate with "leadership" in our country, which includes skills of persuasion, communication, and getting others to follow. Practicing adaptive leadership requires an ability to keep the big picture in view and to subsume one's ego and brilliance in service of engaging the organization's collective brilliance. The answer is not the adaptive leader's biggest contribution, but rather, it's the question – the question that provokes reflection, thought, and engagement. Ideas and innovation can emerge to make progress on these challenges. In practice, the adaptive leader needs to distinguish when leadership is called for and when authority is called for. And that is a function of determining the primary nature of the challenge (technical or adaptive), the elements of each that are present, and using authority or leadership appropriately aligned to the technical and adaptive aspects of the challenge.

Let's take the challenge of COVID-19. As complex as viruses are, the virus itself is a technical challenge. Theoretically, the virus can be addressed by applying knowledge and expertise, as has been done with the development of vaccines. The adaptive aspects of the challenge of COVID-19 are related to issues of values and deep-seated perspectives related to freedom and the perceived loss thereof, perspectives on the role of government, trust or the lack thereof in messengers, messages and mediums, and even political loyalties. There is no "shot" for that and there is no one answer or approach that will "solve" this. Progress will require working on those issues related to the conflict in values and loyalties. What then would an adaptive leadership approach look like? The strength of the adaptive approach is just that – it is adaptive to the unique context and dynamics of a given situation, however, there are core practices and principles we can use. A crisis like COVID-19 understandably will elicit reactive responses and a focus on the immediate needs. Concurrently, this challenge also requires longer range planning and an experimental mindset that can encourage innovative ideas. In addition to identifying the technical and adaptive aspects to challenges, adaptive leaders will "get on the balcony" to look at the situation from a different perspective, recognizing that we all have blind spots based on our existing perspectives and our own values and loyalties that come from our lived experiences.[14] Another important way of eliciting a diversity of perspectives is to invite them from members of your team. How do they see the challenge? How would they approach it? Adaptive leaders have to regulate the level of distress in the organization so that it isn't unbearable but can compel people to action. Adaptive leaders also give the work back to the people, sharing the work of addressing the challenge. They aren't singular heroes. They also say what the team needs to hear rather than what they want to hear. It is keeping an experimental mindset that helps support innovation. We need to note here that none of this is simple or as simple as it may sound. And from a social work education perspective, we approach the training from an ontological framework primarily, as well as an epistemological frame.[15] Leadership is not only learning what to do. It is learning how to be.

Chapter 3 Questions
For Students:

1. How would you describe your own perspective on leadership? What is it? Who is able to exercise leadership?

2. What leadership theories or frameworks have you been exposed to in the course of your education? Other than adaptive leadership, have you studied other forms of leadership – transactional, transformative, status quo, etc.?

3. What is your reaction to some of the adaptive leadership concepts described in this chapter? Do you believe that adaptive leadership theory can contribute to transformative change in human services?

For Educators and Academic Administrators:

1. What are your thoughts about the role of social work schools in preparing students for leadership practice and leadership roles?

2. What resistance might you encounter when adopting an adaptive leadership approach in a university setting?

3. How can schools of social work effectively teach students the principles of adaptive leadership?

Reader's Notes:

CHAPTER 4

STAYING ALIVE AND STAYING TRUE: ETHICS AND FUNDING

Centering Social Work Values in Philanthropy

Times of rapid change require that leaders adapt without losing their "soul," or the values that anchor them to their mission, while also competing for funding. It is clear that leaders cannot take a transactional approach. They must demonstrate the willingness and capacity to engage in potentially uncomfortable conversations about philanthropy. Organizational structures need to incorporate the space for this work to happen if agencies are to truly serve their communities.

The Dilemma of "Good Causes/Bad Money"

Philanthropy has become a huge American enterprise. It always was but recently has grown so that over $410 billion flows into our economy annually.[16] The nonprofit sector is the primary beneficiary, particularly arts institutions, universities, religious institutions, and special interest causes. An example of this relationship is the naming of buildings after wealthy donors or corporations, such as can be seen on hospital wings and more recently charter schools. While the nonprofit sector represents over $1.6 trillion in Gross National Product, philanthropic gifts constitute a growing piece of the pie and often reflect the social interests of large and influential private donors.[15] These donors, some fear, can distort the main purpose or mission of the receiving nonprofit. We will explore these fears and ethical dilemmas.

The nonprofit world is facing an existential dilemma, sometimes referred to as "good causes/bad money." The issue has been given prominence in the nonprofit art and museum world as well as in universities. Many philanthropists who have been funding the cultural arts and university research are also large-scale investors and very often leaders of industries which are acknowledged to be harmful to national or world health. The pharmaceutical industry is one of the most prominent offenders, but other industries engage in major pollution of our cities' waters, emit extreme toxic waste into our air, and manufacture weapons of war. These industries, with their wealthy investors and in some cases private owners, have also been the major contributors to museums, art institutions, music programs, and university research. Some of the very corporations that manufacture products that contribute to ill health and addictions were found to be contributors to university research that aims to alleviate the harmful effects of the very product they have invested in.

Nonprofit organizations have been the beneficiaries of the contributions made by wealthy individuals who in their professional lives have created harmful products. The organizations and universities use their contributions to do good, to engage in basic research, to provide citizen activism, and to redress racial intolerance. Without these contributions these nonprofits would be severely limited in their ability to address these societal issues. The dilemma, however, is real. Can we accept money that will go for good works from individuals or corporations who create and promote products which are harmful, hurtful, and in many instances extremely dangerous?

This situation is not new. For years, many organizations have chosen not to look beyond the contribution or the expressed interest of the donor. Recently, the effort has been to see the donor in his or her totality: where has the money come from, what is the donor's larger intention, does the donation camouflage the donor's larger role? Some have said without such questioning, the nonprofit becomes complicit in actions that are the antithesis of its mission. Some have suggested that our dilemma is nothing more than a mirror of the nature of our capitalist society which pits social obligation against economic gain.

There needs to be much internal reflection about how values and beliefs have central meaning to this process of review. Giving away millions for good causes should not be an entitlement or provide a cover up for otherwise harmful activities. Few industries embody the complexity of this issue more than hospitals.

Case study: Hospitals and the Meaning of "Community Benefit"

Hospitals fall into three financial categories: private hospitals that function as a business, public hospitals owned by state or local governments with the obligation to care for underserved populations, and third, "private nonprofit" hospitals which include more than half of all our hospitals in the U.S. These private nonprofits constitute most of the teaching and research hospitals, such as the Mayo-Clinic, Cleveland Clinic, Johns Hopkins, Mass General, Mt. Sinai, Columbia-Presbyterian, Weill-Cornell, and NYU Langone. These nonprofit hospitals are tax-exempt and pay no local or federal taxes in exchange for providing a "community benefit." Tax exemption is a gift provided by the tax-paying community and should exist only when clearly defined benefits, by way of tangible medical services, are provided for local residents. But a recent study by Politico has shown that these nonprofit hospitals, with their explosive growth, actually show larger "profits or surpluses" than for-profit private hospitals.[17] Philanthropists have provided billions of dollars over the last decade to these nonprofit hospitals, very often carrying their names. Upon examination, these hospitals have provided relatively few free or reduced cost services to local residents, especially those under the poverty line.

When we began this work, the University of Pittsburgh Medical Center was engaged in a lawsuit from the city to revoke its tax exempt status because, in the city's view, the university medical center was not providing a sustained community benefit.[18] The same was true for the Morristown Hospital in New Jersey and a number of other large teaching hospitals throughout our country.[19] Many of these private, nonprofit hospitals are the largest employers in their town or city and have enormous economic bases – that is not to say that the wages paid to their employees, particularly nurses aides, orderlies, porters, and transporters reflect the institutions' understanding of or concern for the well-being of their employees. If nonprofits of any kind, with a tax exemption that benefits both the institution and the donor, do not serve a social purpose, one should question their continued status. (At the time of this writing, the Pittsburgh suit has been settled in favor of the medical center; the settlement in Morristown was settled in favor of the state. Such varying outcomes suggest this important debate is unresolved. [20])

Philanthropy is not to be taken for granted. If we are granting tax exemption to an institution or organization, and if donors are similarly receiving a major tax break by being able to write off their donation, then those institutions have a primary obligation to serve the needs of the community. This is not meant to be a general condemnation of nonprofit hospitals or medical centers. Many are doing absolutely exceptional and needed work, particularly in medical research. But community benefit is the main instrument that, in law and in practice, is the determinant for the provision of tax exemption.

The Limits of Socially Responsible Investing

In nonprofits, fiduciaries are responsible for knowing how the organization's money is invested. Endowments are typically invested in equities in an effort to both grow the endowment for future use and provide income for current operations. Many organizations, in recent years, have found prudent ways to align their financial goals with the values of the organization. This effort has largely been the province of universities and colleges, which have formed a network examining both national and international investments to assure that the companies they invest in are aligned with their values. This initiative has also been given both a voice and influence by large foundations such as Ford, Rockefeller, MacArthur, and Gates. To coincide with this undertaking some of our largest investment conglomerates such as Blackrock, Blackstone, Goldman Sachs, JP Morgan, and UBS have committed to these nonprofits that their investments will be socially responsible and readily available to the investing institutions.

Museums and other arts institutions have recently joined universities in this national effort. The question now raised is not only about endowment investments but about individual donor gifts. Should an institution accept donations to support its "good works" when it is known that the donor has secured funds for that gift through purposes that are not aligned with the organization's values?

Still, thus far human service nonprofits have not had to squarely address this issue. Funds raised were always seen as going toward organizational purposes and programs, and that by itself was sufficient to accept and justify the gift. Now, however, the issue has been elevated to an examination of donors, their beliefs and philosophies, and more importantly the means by which they secured their wealth. This significant dilemma is amplified by the influence donors have over organization's missions, especially in terms of which outcomes are valued. Our perennial challenge is to be able receive the support of a multiplicity of donors while remaining loyal to the values of the profession.

Process Matters: Valuing Inputs and Outputs

In recent years, much attention has been given to the issue of research and evaluation. In fact, social work practice has largely been judged by outcomes achieved rather than the process used to achieve positive outcomes. The standards for examining outcomes have largely been evaluated through "evidence-based practice." Social work organizations have therefore required restructuring to include a research and evaluation component that can systematically review outcomes along more objective, data-guided criteria.

The profession has placed a premium on using scientifically based outcomes in addition to process inputs to examine programs and activities. We have referred to both evidence-based practice and outcome funding as examples of this clear direction. More recently, the external community, principally made up of private and governmental funders, has also attempted to measure the work of nonprofits by a variety of "objective" standards. Other organizations, such as the Better Business Bureau and Charity Navigator, have used more quantitative measures – relative administrative costs versus program costs, dollar distributions, and fundraising costs.[21] Most recently, a new organization by the name of ImpactMatters has attempted to use quantitative measures in a rigorous way to evaluate the validity of work by nonprofits.[22] ImpactMatters is looking at impact through "apples to apples" comparisons of organizations in individual sectors such as food distribution and healthcare. Their effort, of course, is to help donors maximize the effect of their charitable dollars.

While it is recognized that this research orientation is most useful, we also recognize that human relationships are complicated, dynamic, and subjective and cannot always be measured or placed in an operational matrix. Factors leading to positive behavioral change require a full examination of all interventions available, both clinically and scientifically. We have pointed out that much of the work that social service agencies are expected to provide – homeless services, drug and alcohol prevention, improving family interactions and relationships, and providing summer camp to poor children – have great value but are difficult to measure with respect to impact, even utilizing evidence-based approaches. ImpactMatters has identified eight areas where they believe impact, with quantitative measures, can be measured: services to veterans, clean water, homelessness, health, poverty, hunger, education, and climate change. We question whether all of those eight areas are effectively measurable; however, we do not resist the effort to establish better ways for determining the best use of charitable or governmental dollars.

This issue, however, raises a variety of other problematic but important issues. Since the 1980s, many social service agencies, particularly those that are community based, believed that in a pluralistic society, every effort should be made to racially integrate services. One large agency in New York City, The Children's Aid Society, restructured its summer camping services to assure that none of its many camps, both sleepaway and day camps, would be racially segregated, even though the children registered for these camps came from segregated neighborhoods. The agency trained its staff and engaged each community to understand and accept that this was an organizational priority. While the program took some time to develop, over a period of several years, the results were phenomenal.

For the first time a socially integrated group of children experienced one another in natural settings and engaged in all kinds of activities. The parents welcomed the program and indeed it was the first time that many of their children – White, Black, Latino, and Asian – had a chance to connect and learn about one another's culture and history. This begs the question; how do you measure the impact of such a program in quantitative measures? There might be great impact with respect to the individual child's (and parent's) sense of self, of others, and of the community. Each activity and personal interaction are greater than the sum of its parts.

This is a sample of what our democracy is about at its roots. Being able to connect across differences is historically how America has strengthened civil society. Unfortunately, many of the efforts at integration have given way to new concepts, obfuscating the need to integrate by focusing only on more "objective" standards such as "quality education and community engagement." One problem with this is that the focus is limited to a specific community, usually communities of color or of lower economic status. The question for us, however, is what measurement can be applied to programs that are established to engage consumers in ways that help them face the world, develop a sense of self, and visualize the country in broader and more pluralistic ways.

As we explored earlier, the overriding professional social work doctrine today centers around evidence-based practice – notably the capacity to effectively chart needs, services, and interventions along clear markers that result in specific outcomes. One wonders whether or how complicated bio-psycho-social needs can fit neatly into an objective model. The social work profession needs to seriously examine this issue since it now forms the core of so much social work practice. We have not yet resolved the issue of "process versus progress" – what goes into the mix to determine what comes out. Our profession, over many years, has been process–and relationship-oriented. We now must integrate that knowledge with more science and data-oriented outcomes. This complex work will require an honest examination of our practice.

Chapter 4 Questions

For students:

1. How do we present social work values in ways that can be understood by the philanthropic world?

2. How do you feel about the dilemma of "good causes/bad money"? What are your approaches and possible solutions?

3. Should university or agency endowments be invested only in those entities that correspond to the profession's stated values?

For Educators and Academic Administrators:

1. The limits of socially responsible investing present considerable dilemmas. Do you think university policy is ready for a "divestiture" discussion?

2. Do you believe the efforts of the social work profession to focus on practice outcomes and "evidence based practice" has minimized process and the intangibles of change through relationship building?

Reader's Notes:

BOARDS OF DIRECTORS: REPRESENTATION AND ACCOUNTABILITY

The Evolving Role of Boards of Directors

Board composition has always been important but has taken on greater significance in recent years. Social work origins were "citizen and community based" even though those terms were not used in the late nineteenth century. Social work institutions be they settlement houses, homes for people experiencing poverty and homelessness, or visiting nurses, were developed locally, with local governance and largely volunteer leadership and "friendly visitor" staff. Over the years as the social work profession evolved and developed, the governance of these institutions largely remained local with better informed citizens becoming the board members and professionals assuming the roles that volunteers previously exercised.

In the 1930s, social work was a principal profession, emerging to fulfill the roles needed by the community and the larger society to care for the ill, the abandoned, the abused and neglected, the addicted, and the homeless. The governance process also evolved as government regulation began to play a larger role. Additionally, there came a shift with the well-to-do, most often non-local residents, becoming trustees and board members. This was true of both larger institutions like hospitals and smaller community service agencies. Over time, wealthy and concerned citizens, who became known as philanthropists, also became the board decision makers, with trained or untrained social workers in staff positions.

The role and function of boards of directors in nonprofits have changed greatly during the last ten years. About nineteen years ago, the Federal Sarbanes/Oxley Act placed considerably increased obligations on all boards to exercise greater accountability with respect to executive oversight and compensation, self-dealing, and fiscal management. Boards in the corporate sector have faced these obligations in ways that placed greater liability both on themselves and on the corporate structure. While initially nonprofits were exempt from some of the more onerous obligations, they too are now being held to a higher standard of oversight.

Clearly boards could no longer comfortably serve as rubber stamps. While most nonprofit boards are largely unremunerated volunteers, they must assure that their organization meets at least minimum standards of resources, management efficiency, and service outcomes. The role of the CEO or executive director has also changed. While the chief executive still occupies the main management authority, his or her relationship to the board has required greater levels of information sharing and responsibility for agency operations, particularly in the fiscal arena.

Nonprofits, like most organizational structures, are both influenced by and responsive to changes in the larger environment. This includes responding to movements like Black Lives Matter and #MeToo, as well as equal pay and the needs of the LGBTQ community. Nonprofits have an enhanced function and therefore greater community responsibility for ethical conduct. Organizational culture, while always important in the light of corporate malfeasance, is of greater importance today.

Executives as Board Educators

The board as an entity has become much more visible to both government, stakeholders, and the public. In turn, board members have become more sensitized and, in many instances, worried about legal liability if they do not exercise proper supervision. This concern has had unanticipated consequences. While most boards are generally now more aware of agency mission and services, they at times have overstepped the proper boundary between board policy maker and professional implementer. While many executives in nonprofits have often consulted with board leaders on matters such as law, media, real estate, and insurance, they have on occasion sought advice on professional practice issues which can be counterproductive. An example of this misuse of collaboration would be an executive seeking board agreement on whether the professional staff should outreach to community members being denied services elsewhere. Especially in times of increased risk and liability, executives must be ever mindful of sharing the information with the board and not abdicating professional responsibility to make practice-related decisions.

Boards have a proper, important, and in many instances, a vital role in the functioning and survival of the nonprofit. However, their role must be strategic and less tactical. The professional, executive leadership maintains a critical role as the main policy implementer and board educator. The professional must keep the board informed and abreast of all new developments, even and perhaps especially when sharing unpleasant information. Programmatic failures do not mean that hard work and effort were not applied to achieve a positive outcome or that important learning hasn't occurred. Boards need to understand that a good portion of our work has been untested and sometimes resembles more of a "clinical trial" than an evidence-based intervention. Sharing is not only for "good news and positive experiences."

In order for the agency professional to be the principal educator she must feel secure in her position and sufficiently knowledgeable to respond to queries and questions that may arise from the shared information. The key to the board-professional relationship rests in an open and trusting arrangement with a clear understanding of the differences in role and function. Boards generally expect the executive to exercise sound judgement, strong leadership, and a willingness to take responsibility for her decision making. The executive, in turn, must continuously direct the board's priorities toward social work values, especially in the realm of representation.

Representation as a Living Practice

Today social workers largely fulfill the service provision and clinical roles in nonprofits. In large social service agencies, businesspeople, other wealthy individuals, and legacy families become the trustees. We now recognize that this separation can constitute a disjunction. Institutions, while constantly in need of resources, must also represent the consumer with the distance between the provider and the consumer narrowing. Those nonprofits that maintain a visible distance between those who support the institution and those who receive the benefit from the institution have a responsibility to reduce that distance. Participatory action research and advocacy is one way to include clients and increase their voice and their presence in leadership positions. Consumers throughout our country want a say in what services they receive and want efficacy in their own actions.

Representation should no longer be a theoretical term or an isolated initiative but a living practice that is embedded throughout organizational practices.

Our boards must reflect the community as well as be responsive to the organization's financial interests and management. If the board composition is too removed from the needs of the constituents, a schism is created. We cannot encourage a system of haves serving have nots. We must strive to remove obstacles within these social sectors and have the vision and courage to change policies that affect the total environment.

Chapter 5 Questions

For Students:

1. What have you learned about the legal and policy role of boards of directors of institutions that are nonprofit and tax exempt?

2. Have you ever been provided an opportunity to appear at a board meeting or meet the members of the boards of directors?

3. Have you witnessed any involvement of trustees in the university or at agencies?

4. From your observation, do trustees appear to represent the full spectrum of the community? Why is this important?

For Educators and Academic Administrators:

1. Have senior faculty been periodically invited to attend and/or participate in trustee or board meetings?

2. Should universities and agencies include social work professionals as equal members of the board?
If so, are there inherent conflicts?

3. Has our profession sufficiently advocated
for board representation of the consumer or student populations?

Reader's Notes:

PART III
EDUCATION AND PRACTICE

CHAPTER 6

THE CASE FOR POLYMATHIC CURRICULA IN SOCIAL WORK EDUCATION

The Need to Prepare Social Workers for Executive Roles

T he social work profession is at a crossroads. The pandemic and racial justice movements are a clarion call for agencies to reinvigorate their roles as advocates and change agents. New influencers will be called upon to help the nonprofit sector navigate these turbulent times. We need to ensure these new leaders include social work professionals who are equipped to step into executive positions. The current social work education model needs to be re-examined and bolstered to activate this outcome.

In recent years the social services community has experienced a significant rise in non-social workers trained in different disciplines, principally law, public administration, social policy, and education, who have been employed as executive managers in nonprofits. Many of these individuals have found a professional home in organizations previously led by social workers. While this ever-growing group has brought to organizations their unique training and discipline, they have only a cursory knowledge of both the history and practice of social welfare and social work. Our concern is that the services that organizations administer, over time, may lose or dilute their focus on core social work values – self-determination, individual rights, social equality, cultural identity, and social action.[23]

This separation needs to be addressed not only by social service nonprofits and their boards but social work education itself. The curricula in schools of social work needs to focus more on leadership development and also provide more context and opportunity for students to choose a direction that can realistically lead to executive leadership. Schools of social work also need to examine the credentials of their faculty with respect to background and skill sets to enable effective teaching in executive leadership.

In this regard, we strongly recommend that schools of social work reexamine their curricula to assure that courses are available for those students who have an interest in executive management and leadership. Such curricula and programs existed throughout the 1960s and 1970s. This resulted in many social service agencies, particularly those serving communities of need, being staffed at all levels, from the executive to service providers, with social work trained personnel. This model changed when the field of social work turned almost exclusively toward the behavioral sciences. While the curricula worked for many, it omitted a focus on management, organizational development, leadership, and community organizing. It is most important for this trend to be reversed. While we acknowledge that most social workers still will be trained as clinicians and practitioners, a significant number will also find a home in the administrative and executive leadership modalities. This will ensure, over time, the continuation of social work ethics, values, and culture, which are the life stream for agencies serving the communities of greatest need.

Institute in Interdisciplinary Polymathic Studies

While our effort is directed toward an enlarged social work curricula, including a significant concentration on social reform, advocacy, community organization, activism, and most importantly executive leadership, we also recognize that most agency executives are currently not social work trained. We are, therefore, embarking on a two-step reconfiguration that focuses on the need to train social workers for such positions and at the same time offer those in the disciplines of law, education, public administration, and business training an opportunity to learn and be exposed to social work values and principles.

The approach we are suggesting is a joint academy or institute in interdisciplinary polymathic studies that introduces collective ideas for problem solving that enhance critical thinking. Universities have long organized their curricula into silos: medicine separated from political science, art from engineering, social work from public health, law from social work. While a number of universities have established joint or dual-degrees the silos nevertheless remain intact. Polymathic study is a novel learning environment that assembles the ingenuity of a community of learners and teachers leading to sound critical judgment and enhanced wisdom.

Ten years ago, the University of Southern California established an academy for polymathic studies that nurtures this new manner of scholarship to give students from various disciplines a chance to bring their knowledge and skills together to address and solve social problems. Schools of social work would make an enormous contribution if they developed a similar academy and drew into it, with university sanction, students from the disciplines of law, public health, education, and public policy who expect to enter the nonprofit world. Social work would influence the process and venture beyond the confines of any one discipline.

This process builds on the creation of cross-disciplinary research including biomedical/neuroscience, the humanities, public health, and social science. Each discipline within this polymath would learn much about the other disciplines and develop a fuller understanding of the response to human need. On a societal level, many of the most challenging issues of our time would benefit enormously from exploration and a commitment to praxis, a synthesis of practice and theory.

Sidney Harman, the innovator of the polymath academy at USC, described this new way of thinking as asynchronous and multi-disciplinary.[24] If schools of social work would consider the establishment of an interdisciplinary polymathic approach, we would be providing our field with an enormous step forward – educating those presently not social work trained with a fuller understanding of the world they are inhabiting.

This two-step approach, executive leadership training of social work students and the inclusion of students in other disciplines in a polymathic interdisciplinary institute, will result in more effective leadership in the nonprofit world. Schools of social work would be playing the leadership role within the academy in forging this alliance for people who will ultimately end up in the same arena. This will help future agency leaders develop a greater appreciation and comprehension of the culture, knowledge, skills, and values embodied in social work, including its history, culture, and philosophy.

The first step would be the convening of a group of academics and field leaders to work through a consensus of the value of a polymathic approach, the inclusion of an institute as an accepted part of their respective school structure, and then the development of a two-semester curricula that includes interdisciplinary theory, knowledge, and practice. This is the first of many steps needed to develop a workforce to fulfill current leadership needs and, in all likelihood, the expanding need in the future. For this polymathic institute to be successful, all participating schools must assign or recruit the most experienced instructors who can integrate knowledge in effective teaching modules. Field placement and executive modeling should be a part of this experience.

We have to expand our academic sequence to recognize the reality of shared leadership in the nonprofit arena. We propose that under the aegis of schools of social work, we train and educate students in law, public policy, and education.

1. *Schools of social work should incorporate into their curricula leadership courses with concentrations in management, workforce development, governance, budgeting, strategic planning, and community building.*

2. *Schools of social work should recruit faculty capable of teaching, by example and experience, the executive functions of running a social service agency.*

3. *Schools of social work should do extensive outreach to community agencies, especially those already affiliated with the school, to develop and offer executive leadership programs in conjunction with the agency and its social work staff.*

4. *Efforts should be made to invite board members and trustees to institutes and programs that orient and educate social work students.*

5. *Transitional steps need to be incorporated in social service agencies to assure that when executive positions are open, existing social work staff with specific management skills and leadership training have an opportunity to secure a high-level administrative or executive position.*

6. *Schools of social work and human service agencies should form a collaborative, ongoing effort to ensure that, over time, positions of leadership in nonprofit organizations are filled by social-work trained personnel.*

Chapter 6 Questions
For Students, Educators, and Academic Administrators:

1. Do you think that a polymathic approach within a school of social work would have value for the profession? Would it enhance our leadership position within the community and the political sphere?

2. Do you think the two-step approach toward leadership, broadening our base, and at the same time focusing leadership within the social work curricula, makes good sense?

3. How do we educate university administrators and funders to better understand the history, values, and ethics of the social work profession?

Reader's Notes:

Reflections from Dr. Michael A. Lindsey

Michael A. Lindsey, PhD, MSW, MPH, is the Executive Director of the McSilver Institute for Poverty Policy and Research and the Constance and Martin Silver Professor of Poverty Studies at NYU's Silver School of Social Work. As an institute executive and scholar of child and adolescent mental health, Dr. Lindsey is uniquely positioned to discuss the role that social work plays in shaping policy.

Question 1: Since assuming the Directorship of the McSilver Institute, what have you learned with respect to integrating policy and research to influence social work practice?

Dr. Michael Lindsey: First, I have learned that policy is not a rational, linear process. It takes strong science but that is not enough. You also need powerful storytelling to appeal to emotions. I have a recent example of how powerful storytelling and strong science can help shape the conceptualization of policy. As part of my work at the McSilver Institute, I have been involved in research focusing on mental health treatment disparities related to the circumstances of ethnic minority youth. Black adolescents have been my group of focus. From 1991 to 2017, we have observed a rising trend of suicidal behaviors among Black adolescents as well as among Black 5 to 12 year olds. Black youth are the only group to see a rising trend in suicide attempts over that time and have the highest rates of death related to suicide. Also, Black adolescent boys saw a rising trend in terms of having an injury related to a suicide attempt. Suicide attempts rose by 73 percent for Black adolescents and injury attempts rose by 122 percent for Black adolescent boys. That becomes part of the narrative that begins to shape the potential for a policy focus.

I had an opportunity in December of 2018 to do a Congressional briefing on this issue. Prior to the briefing, I huddled with my colleagues at the McSilver Institute. They counseled, "Michael, when you do this briefing, why don't we use this as an opportunity to call on Congress members to establish an emergency task force to address this issue?" I have to credit Rose Pierre-Louis, our Chief Operating Officer, for putting that bug in my ear. So, in the Congressional briefing, I said, "Listen, this is a 'ring the alarm' moment and we need to have an emergency task force, convened by Congress, to begin to look at this issue and decide what kinds of legislation might be brought forth to address it."

Congresswoman Bonnie Watson Coleman heard this clarion call. In January 2019, she contacted me to say, "I want to take you up on that recommendation you offered to establish an emergency task force. I'm going to talk with the Congressional Black Caucus and the Chairwoman, Karen Bass, to see if this might be something that we could take on." The following month, we received an official notification that the Congressional Black Caucus was willing to establish the task force. Then, in April 2019, the task force officially launched with Michael Lindsey as Chair of the working group of experts tasked with conducting background research and shaping a policy focus. This is a process where research is starting to inform policy and has the potential to influence social work practice.

Congresswoman Bonnie Watson Coleman said to me, "Michael, I need a report, so you and your group need to work on a report that will be due to me in December 2019." I replied, "Congresswoman, with all due respect, don't you get a year at least to work on a report of this magnitude?"

She responded, "Not in this instance. I have a game plan and I need you to get this group together and work on this report to be submitted to me in December." So, my McSilver Institute colleagues and I, along with the members of the working group of experts from around the country, rolled our sleeves up and submitted the report to the Congressional Black Caucus by their deadline. I didn't realize that the Congresswoman's game plan was to take this report and make it the basis for a Bill, H.R. 5469 The Pursuing Equity in Mental Health Bill or Act of 2020, that would be sponsored by Congresswoman Bonnie Watson Coleman and members of the Congressional Black Caucus. I am so pleased to announce that at the time of this publication the House of Representatives and the U.S. Congress passed this Bill, which calls for the provision of $108 million to be infused into mental health systems, demonstration projects, and the training and hiring of culturally competent professionals, all in the space of addressing the rising rate of suicide engagement and suicide behaviors among Black youth.

I think this powerfully demonstrates how policy and research inform each other. We had to do the research to inform the policy. And it was critical to tell the story of how young Black people more than any other racial and ethnic group were engaging in suicide behaviors over the course of the last 15 to 25 years. In the report, we described some of the factors that underlie these rising trends that relate to implicit biases. We think that happens starting in schools. Some research has indicated as early as Pre-K that Black kids are suspended or expelled from school because of implicit biases relative to White youth. If these kids are being suspended and expelled from schools at disproportionate rates, then they're not likely to have access to mental health providers or behavioral health support that would keep them connected and engaged in schools in positive ways. Or, we find that in underserved ethnic minority communities, there are not the requisite behavioral health supports and services in schools or practitioners of color who might make it more appealing for a Black family to connect to services. Those are practice issues that need to be substantiated or documented with respect to research; research that we've been doing, that I've been doing in this space. And then it's not enough to do the research, publish it in a high-impact journal, and rest on your laurels. One of the main themes of my leadership of the McSilver Institute is taking knowledge and information and doing more than just publishing it and writing the next grant. We have a responsibility to do something about it.

This is where storytelling becomes especially salient. I have sat across from a parent who has lost their child unfortunately to death by suicide. I've heard their painstaking recount of the day, the hour, the moment they discovered their child had died. And those stories grip my heart. They tear away at the emotional fabric of my being and make me fully charged to do something about it. Not just investigate, interrogate, and answer from a practice perspective; it's not just a clinical issue. It's how we compel the hearts and minds of our elected officials at the federal level to take action. Now, I am hopeful that the Senate and ultimately the President will agree with the House. That is our legislative process, but the wheels of justice are turning toward the realities and the circumstances of Black youth relative to their mental health. To me that is the essence of how research, policy, and practice all come together.

Question 2: What challenges do you face in running a complex policy and research institute within the framework of a clinically-oriented school of social work?

Dr. Michael Lindsey: The question of how we influence clinical practice is always at the forefront of our minds. We have a bottom line at the McSilver Institute to bring in grant dollars to support our work. Most of the work we're grant-funded to do has a clinical perspective. However, it's my conviction that we cannot think about our work in an insular way. We have to dissuade ourselves from being solely focused on the individual and their symptoms. We don't want to rush to address their issues without much reflection and effort put toward the macro-level circumstances that shape their lives.

The challenge for us is to think along a parallel track about how to disseminate our work beyond publications. And so, we use social media platforms and community-based symposia. We engage key stakeholders including elected officials and talk about issues, everything from suicide to completing the Census to the rising digital divide, particularly in light of COVID-19 and the implications it has had on remote learning and remote working. We hold convenings in community spaces to ensure that stakeholders are involved. It's parallel; we have to do both. The conviction and burden is to take both a clinical focus and consider how to address structural and systemic issues. That's what we are trying to do as part of our mission and focus.

Question 3: What do you think NYU Silver should continue to do to better recruit Black, Indigenous, and other People of Color (BIPOC) as faculty and students?

Michael Lindsey: Schools of social work have to focus on the pipeline and how best to build our recruitment efforts to ensure that people from marginalized communities are among the faculty and students. This notion that "if you build it, they will come" is not enough anymore because those kinds of concepts have inherent biases within them, particularly related to where and how you communicate these opportunities and who has access to this information.

You have to be intentional about the importance of recruiting individuals from marginalized communities. Committees that are a part of hiring faculty or interviewing students have to think about the places to best target appeals and opportunities. And, you have to create an environment that is welcoming. If I am a Black person coming to the school potentially as a student or a faculty member,

I will want to know the representation of Black students or Black faculty. What kind of experiences have they had relative to being Black in that school? And if I have any hint or observation that the experiences for Black people have not been good, then it's going to make me incredibly suspicious and cautious about whether that school is right for me.

There's also inner work, if you will, that has to be done. And, you have to do the external work of strategically going to places where you can recruit folks from marginalized communities. For example, we have a whole record of historically Black colleges and universities that are a strong recruitment source. There are also numerous programs that target ethnic minority faculty that might be tapped. So, we cannot rest on this laurel that "it's here, we put out an announcement, people are going to come to it." No, it takes more due diligence than that.

Question 4: How can a school of social work foster an integrated, equitable, and inclusive culture for BIPOC faculty and students?

Dr. Michael Lindsey: There are a number of ways that a school of social work can foster a more integrated, equitable, and inclusive culture. One is through curriculum. Coursework, assignments, and readings should reflect this perspective in every class, not just in classes that focus exclusively on issues of diversity. If faculty have to convene to decide on content areas that should be reflected across the curriculum, then we should do that.

Secondly, faculty meetings should be a place where faculty come together to discuss these issues as they pertain to the curriculum. While each content area may already have a committee, I think we should come together across content areas and talk as a faculty community. This would give faculty an opportunity to work on themselves and to work out their challenges relative to these issues.

I also think having a diverse faculty composition plays a huge role. You can't just talk about these issues in theory but you have to practice them. When you have faculty that reflect diversity, equity, and inclusion, then it conveys the meaningfulness of this perspective to the entire school community. We have to create opportunities for faculty who represent communities of color and communities of diversity; we have to recruit those individuals into our schools in specialized ways. We can't just sit with the standard search processes that are bereft with biases.

Question 5: How has the McSilver Institute influenced the University and the surrounding community toward having a greater understanding of poverty, culture, and race, and the need to engage in social action?

Dr. Michael Lindsey: Let's start with the mission of the McSilver Institute, which is focused on addressing the root causes and consequences of poverty, applying evidence-based interventions or strategies to address these challenges, and translating all of this into action. This relates to our continued research, which aims to develop and disseminate new knowledge that can lead to policy in action. With this mission in mind, I think we are influencing others in a few ways.

First, you can't have a conversation about poverty without talking about how race is inextricably linked to poverty. We're unapologetic about the importance of race to the conversation on poverty, culture, and inequality. We're not afraid to convene conversations on, for example, the 1619 project and our hosting of Nikole Hannah-Jones, who created this project from her purview as a reporter at the New York Times. We had that conversation on campus to talk about the ways in which attitudes and perspectives that led to the enslavement of Blacks continue to perpetuate in our society in a present day context, or the matter of reparations and what is owed to Blacks and communities that have been historically marginalized.

Another example is how we brought Mehrsa Baradaran to campus. She wrote the book, *The Color of Money: Black Banks and the Racial Wealth Gap*, which uses Black banking as a portal to examine the systemic forces that have impeded Black communities' economic success. We invited city officials to participate in this discussion. We want to make sure that we not only convene these perspectives, but we incorporate them into our work.

Additionally, I think we talk about persistent inequalities in a number of ways, including how women of color are often marginalized in leadership roles. One of the things I made a point of focusing on as head of the McSilver Institute is the importance of incorporating women of color leaders into strategic roles that foster our mission-driven activities. We try to mirror what great opportunities are possible when you have a focus on cultivating diverse leadership. In those ways, we try to lead by example as an institute that can create discourse that is action-oriented in terms of the policies and practices that we produce.

PART IV
REFLECTIONS
FROM SOCIAL
WORK EXECUTIVES

We interviewed a cross-section of social work executives to ascertain their views on both their work and the environment that affects their agencies' objectives. The respondents had the opportunity to share concerns that go beyond the questions posed.

William (Bill) Weisberg
Executive Director
Forestdale
67-35 112th Street Forest Hills, NY 11375

Question: The role of the boards of directors/trustees has changed since the crash of 2008 and the impact of new restrictive governmental regulations. Concomitant to that, have these changes adversely affected the role of the CEO and/or the direction and purpose of your agency?

Bill Weisberg: Boards have long been composed of individuals of means. What is new is the increased wealth in New York City after the rebound from the 2008 Recession. Boards are more aware that if things go wrong, they are liable. This makes them tend toward being more conservative, which is not a bad thing. Board oversight is increasingly important in these times as is humility—to know what you don't know. There's a tendency to think the most important aspects of nonprofit governance fall under those areas, such as finances, they know well. So, it becomes important for board members not to make the mistake of thinking that fundraising and finances are more important than the quality of work being provided.

Question: The funding environment has changed since the 2008 Great Recession. How has that impacted your agency's work and priorities?

Bill Weisberg: There is great focus on tracking what is going on in services. This is quite important but doesn't guarantee that all is well. This is in part an influence of using corporate tools and emphases on numbers and metrics as a way to see impact. There does seem to be a belief in the sector that the more corporate-like the sector is, the better. The challenge is to recognize that all of the focus on metrics and corporate management approaches cannot ensure quality practice. Ultimately, practice drives outcomes so it's important to invest and pay close a attention to practice and to quality of services.

Question: In light of today's political and social environment, has your agency increased its focus on advocacy and social reform? What other impacts are your agency and the sector experiencing in the current political and social environment? In what ways has the political environment affected your agency's policies and client needs? Has it affected your relationship with government agencies?

Weisberg: There is increased work in advocacy and social reform in the sector as the hostility toward those perceived to be "others" has increased. Racial justice and equity work has increased, and the New York Community Trust is doing a racial equity lab of which Forestdale is part. Expressions of racism have gone from being more "underground" to more overt in the country and agencies must be more explicit about their values and commitments in this area.

Government regulations have intensified but the public sector does not necessarily understand what it takes to do the work well. But, in New York City there has been an increase in funding for services through tax revenues. There has been a greater investment in thoughtful support for families, which is paying off in better outcomes. There have been some big wins — increased preventive services, reduced foster care census, a higher high school graduation rate, and more early childhood programs. This is going in the right direction and we need more.

Question: You have likely heard about the reduction in social work trained/credentialed leaders in the human services nonprofit arena. Has that concerned you and/or affected the leadership in your organization? What is your perspective on causes, effects, and remedies?

Weisberg: It does seem to be accurate that fewer agency executives are social workers. Even supervisors are less likely to be MSW credentialed and come from related fields such as school counseling and public administration. There's an observable decline in rigorous clinical training among social work school graduates. Their training may be more diversified and yet their clinical training is not preparing them as well for the work as was the case a couple of decades ago. This is compounded by caseworkers having to do so many concrete tasks. If the trend of more staff and leaders from related fields continues, one thought is to offer a one-year intensive post-graduate certificate program, like a boot-camp, in child development and family systems work.

Phoebe Boyer
President and Chief Executive Officer
Children's Aid
117 West 124th Street, 3rd Floor New York, NY 10027

Question: The role of the boards of directors/trustees has changed since the crash of 2008 and the impact of new restrictive governmental regulations. Concomitant to that, have these changes adversely affected the role of the CEO and/or the direction and purpose of your agency?

Phoebe Boyer: The biggest shift is that boards have a greater sense of understanding of the way finances work and their own responsibility. They understand the differences between management and governance. There is a sense that the sector is fragile given government contracts, and this is largely good because these contracts don't cover full costs. They are more understanding of how this impacts agencies.

In terms of board composition, there's a focus on a range of skill sets, such as technology and finance, and a better reflection of the staff and the clients served. Still, we need fundraisers on boards and people with networks especially given the wild policy shifts.

Question: In light of today's political and social environment, has your agency increased its focus on advocacy and social reform? What other impacts are your agency and the sector experiencing in the current political and social environment? In what ways has the political environment affected your agency's policies and client needs?

Phoebe Boyer: CAS has a sizable policy and advocacy division. They have an entire team training young people and parents, which is critical to changing policy and advocating for funding. Because CAS' work operates across systems, CAS uses that and leverages different dollars. They have to think through master contracts rather than many teeny grants.

Question: The funding environment has changed since the 2008 Great Recession. How has that impacted your agency's work and priorities?

Phoebe Boyer: There is a greater focus on outcomes. That is creating some positive changes, including a more honest dialogue about the real challenges of delivering services. For example, The Nonprofit Resiliency Committee, a coalition of New York City-based health and human service nonprofits, is engaging in conversations around indirect costs, their impact on the agency, and their effect on service delivery. The government and the provider sector were not having this type of conversation before.

On the other hand, the greater focus on outcomes has an oppressive side. It's a constant Catch 22. Technology and training are essential to collect and analyze data but how many agencies have this capacity? How many funders pay for this capacity? It's important to be clear with funders about what we can and cannot measure and put our focus on outcomes rather than outputs. The better we can demonstrate our outcomes, the better we can leverage more adequate and sustainable funding, including master contracts.

Question: How has your agency responded to the current conversation on diversity, equity and inclusion and the need for anti-racist approaches? How have these conversations affected the sector?

Phoebe Boyer: The leadership team is wrestling with this issue and its many different approaches and perspectives. The guiding principle is embedded in it; don't make it a separate program or initiative. They are wrestling with definitions. Clarity on this is essential. These issues are very complicated for leadership now. It's tied to the political climate. Their work is breaking down barriers and everyone wants them to respond to everything.

There's also the challenge of balancing the need for transparency in a highly litigious environment in which you're running complex initiatives. While it is true that change is a constant, we are experiencing a very rapid rate of change on many levels. It is a challenge to be proactive rather than reactive with this extremely rapid pace of change. It is tough to plan for even 6 to 18 months. Governmental instability can mean loss of contracts when administrations change.

There are increased risks to be managed: social media surfacing problem behavior with staff members, insurance companies are more skittish about ensuring and screening, and onboarding staff is more expensive.

Ricardo (Ric) Estrada
President and Chief Executive Officer
Metropolitan Family Services
One North Dearborn, Suite 1000 Chicago, IL 60602

Question: The role of the boards of directors/trustees has changed since the crash of 2008 and the impact of new restrictive governmental regulations. Concomitant to that, have these changes adversely affected the role of the CEO and/or the direction and purpose of your agency?

Ric Estrada: Board composition has remained consistent over the years with mostly corporate civic leaders who care about their communities. Some boards have diversified in terms of race and ethnicity.

Question: How has your agency responded to the current conversation on diversity, equity and inclusion and the need for anti-racist approaches? How have these conversations affected the sector?

Ric Estrada: These are very important issues, especially to millennials, and the demand for change is urgent and there is little patience for the time it takes. There is a strong effort to unionize nonprofits. The diversity, equity, and inclusion issues are prominent in philanthropy, with many philanthropic organizations being less diverse. This creates a tension, an "us vs. them" tension, where agencies feel that philanthropy wants their projects carried out but doesn't really understand the work.

Nonprofits do find themselves having to engage in more advocacy in the current political climate. There is more tension for human service nonprofits whose boards may have many politically right-leaning individuals and yet the agencies are engaging in challenging policymakers and administration officials from the right. This has to be handled carefully and skillfully, tying it to the sustainability of the agency and the mission.

Question: You have likely heard about the reduction in social work trained/credentialed leaders in the human services nonprofit arena. Has that concerned you and/or affected the leadership in your organization? What is your perspective on causes, effects and remedies?

Ric Estrada: MFS considers itself a true social work organization where a social work degree is needed to rise through the ranks. The CEO, COO, and Executive Director all hold MSWs. It's controversial not to have one. I also pursued an MBA to bolster my credibility as someone who could manage. It mattered to the board as the social work degree did not address their questions as to whether I could help the organization grow financially.

I see shifts in which individuals with law degrees and other credentials are increasingly running human services nonprofits and business schools are training people to be nonprofit leaders. Some of those trained go on to be Vice Presidents of Human Resources but many aren't satisfied with that role – they aspire to lead human services nonprofits. It is my assessment that the shrinking pool of nonprofit CEOs with MSWs is not just in New York City but is a trend in Chicago and beyond. It is encouraged by business and philanthropy, especially for bigger agencies.

I favor the MSW for nonprofit human services leaders because of the practice experience that is foundational to the degree in the form of rigorous field placements and the greater consciousness of all of the complex issues involved in the systems perspective.

David Jones

President and Chief Executive Officer

Community Service Society

633 Third Ave, 10th FL New York, NY 10017

Question: The role of the boards of directors/trustees has changed since the crash of 2008 and the impact of new restrictive governmental regulations. Concomitant to that, have these changes adversely affected the role of the CEO and/or the direction and purpose of your agency?

David Jones: Boards of directors and trustees have become more concerned with financial management and increased responsibility for the functioning of the nonprofit. While this may be helpful in many instances, boards need to support the professional and efforts to render a needed service. Boards also need continuous "professional education" to understand the functioning of the nonprofit and the development of sound leadership transition planning.

Question: In light of today's political and social environment, has your agency increased its focus on advocacy and social reform? What other impacts are your agency and the sector experiencing in the current political and social environment? In what ways has the political environment affected your agency's policies and client needs?

David Jones: The nonprofit sector is less dependent on the government for financial support than in the past. While this can create less dependency, it was more a reaction to the succession of mayors who did not fully appreciate the work of the nonprofit sector as service provider, advocate, and critic. The sector is under attack by right-wing forces nationally and locally and has suffered under the constraints imposed upon it by various levels of government. One can see this most clearly in the healthcare sector, particularly both governmental and ultra-conservative responses to Planned Parenthood and other reproductive health services. Because of this present detachment, the sector needs, more than ever, to ensure its own survival and independence by building an endowment and reserve funds so that its work can continue even if the government cuts back or eliminates its support. While direct services are the primary victim of government reductions, research and evaluation dollars have also been severely cut. Our opportunity for innovation and experimentation based upon our research and clinical trials is under attack.

While the tendency of many in the nonprofit sector is to keep a low profile, our approach should be, more than ever, on advocacy, social change and, where necessary, resistance. It may be that our efforts in New York should shift more to the state and city council, if the more traditional sources of government support tend to be more resistant. This is particularly true in the healthcare arena.

Question: You have likely heard about the reduction in social work trained/credentialed leaders in the human services nonprofit arena. Has that concerned you and/or affected the leadership in your organization? What is your perspective on causes, effects and remedies?

David Jones: Schools of social work have an important role in the provision of both sound practitioners, particularly in the social reform arena, and in the development of public, private, and university coalitions. Graduate students in law and public policy may also need additional training in understanding the functions of social welfare and social work.

Evelyn J. Diaz
President
Heartland Alliance
208 S. LaSalle Street, Suite 1300, Chicago, IL 60604

Question: The role of the boards of directors/trustees has changed since the crash of 2008 and the impact of new restrictive governmental regulations. Concomitant to that, have these changes adversely affected the role of the CEO and/or the direction and purpose of your agency?

Evelyn Diaz: Transparency allows the board to be more strategic and less tactical. Executives should value board members' time and allow space for generative conversation. Boards will always need people with resources and that will remain true in the coming years but depending on the organizational priorities, board members may also be asked to provide needed expertise.

Heartland Alliance is comprised of five companies, each with its own board. It is a challenge for organizations with complicated structures to see themselves as one organization and one board.

Question: The funding environment has changed since the 2008 Great Recession. How has that impacted your agency's work and priorities?

Evelyn Diaz: A common theme is that there is an expectation of investors that organizations consistently evolve to demonstrate their impact. Indeed, "change is the sea we swim in." The pace at which change is happening is so fast and they have noticed that government, private, and individual funders are approaching their work differently. They want to know that their dollars are having a specific impact

— a return on investment on steroids. We must understand data more deeply and collect it more systematically. What is challenging is that organizations are not equipped to do this and funders don't pay for it. We need that skill set on staff. Fewer people are making more decisions on what programs are valuable. Corporate values are dominating.

Question: In light of today's political and social environment, has your agency increased its focus on advocacy and social reform? What other impacts are your agency and the sector experiencing in the current political and social environment? In what ways has the political environment affected your agency's policies and client needs?

Evelyn Diaz: The current political environment is really affecting us. The zero tolerance policy at the border has led to packed shelters. Our agency has become a lightning rod for anger and rage toward the administration. The current political environment has posed reputational risks. It's "the curse that keeps on giving." We are still being protested by groups. As new policies are enacted by the administration, we are in the position of receiving funds and suing the government at the same time. We have to continue to bear it. This is something that agencies are facing as they are both contractors of the government and also must advocate for their clients.

Question: How has your agency responded to the current conversation on diversity, equity and inclusion and the need for anti-racist approaches? How have these conversations affected the sector?

Evelyn Diaz: We have little board diversity and funders have issues with that. In years past, the conversation on this issue was a "check the box" approach. What is really needed is a culture shift where everyone feels like they belong and like it's their organization. The board is trying to be more reflective of their clients.

Question: You have likely heard about the reduction in social work trained/credentialed leaders in the human services nonprofit arena. Has that concerned you and/or affected the leadership in your organization? What is your perspective on causes, effects and remedies?

Evelyn Diaz: In Chicago, major nonprofits are still helmed by social workers, but I don't think this will remain the case. It's not that social workers aren't respected but in bigger, more complex organizations, there will be more non-social workers hired. For example, our new executive team includes no social workers. They came from the private sector because their experience in changing complex organizations was needed. So far, I've observed no problems with their connecting to the mission, but they have been unprepared for how under-resourced the sector is. It's a total culture shock.

Sharon Osborne

Former President and Chief Executive Officer

Children's Home Society

12360 Lake City Way N.E., Suite 450, Seattle, WA 98125

Question: The role of the boards of directors/trustees has changed since the crash of 2008 and the impact of new restrictive governmental regulations. Concomitant to that, have these changes adversely affected the role of the CEO and/or the direction and purpose of your agency?

Sharon Osborne: The board, which is spread throughout the state of Washington and represents many different constituencies, is currently engaged in significant strategic planning to prepare for the next five years. The success of the strategic planning consortium following the last Great Recession resulted in an increase of over 25% in private giving for the operational budget.

Question: In light of today's political and social environment, has your agency increased its focus on advocacy and social reform? What other impacts are your agency and the sector experiencing in the current political and social environment? In what ways has the political environment affected your agency's policies and client needs? Has it affected your relationship with government agencies?

Sharon Osborne: Ideally, the public sector should get out of direct services and support the work of the nonprofit, human services sector. Many agencies have to spend a lot of time educating public and government funding sources to help them understand the value of family-focused community based services. It is an ongoing effort to assure contin-ued funding for vital services.

Question: You have likely heard about the reduction in so-cial work trained/credentialed leaders in the human services nonprofit arena. Has that concerned you and/or affected the leadership in your organization? What is your perspec-tive on causes, effects and remedies?

Sharon Osborne: There is a dearth of people who want to or who have the requisite preparation to assume CEO roles in human services agencies. Developing talent from within is optimal when possible. You don't have to have an MBA but you must know the business side and hire people who do know it.

Bill Baccaligni

President and Chief Executive Officer

The New York Foundling

590 Avenue of the Americas, NY, NY 10011 Chelsea

Question: The role of the boards of directors/trustees has changed since the crash of 2008 and the impact of new restrictive governmental regulations. Concomitant to that, have these changes adversely affected the role of the CEO and/or the direction and purpose of your agency? Do you see any trends in the sector following the Recession?

Bill Baccaglini: Our board at the Foundling, while still committed to the care of the most vulnerable children, has embraced this new focus on primary prevention and agency outreach. The board understands that it can afford to be less risk-averse based upon our assessment of need and the development of independent financial resources that will enable us to not be as dependent or subjected to government whims. Most agencies, I fear, are not fully ready for this change but understand that the change is upon us.

Clearly, there is a decreasing present need for residential care. This affects many agencies who for years reserved beds for residential use. The effort today is much more on prevention, home care, and community outreach. Many agencies, including the Foundling, have expanded their mission to include a focus on primary education and charter schools.

The role of welfare, while still important, has now been enlarged to focus on the long-term educational needs of children, particularly those who are most vulnerable and in greatest need. Our focus for too long has been on the immediate, "putting out fires" and being too apologetic for not getting to the more fundamental basic needs of children. Charter schools are one way to exercise this primary responsibility.

Question: You have likely heard about the reduction in social work trained/credentialed leaders in the human services nonprofit arena. Has that concerned you and/or affected the leadership in your organization? What is your perspective on causes, effects and remedies?

Bill Baccaglini: Unfortunately, there is a shortage of good, well-trained personnel to reach the many needs of the communities we serve. Schools of social work must also see this new social context and have a greater appreciation of community issues and social reform. Schools of social work must build their curricula around advocacy, legal constraints, and board development. To do so is not mission abandonment but rather an understanding of a present need for diversity and institutional change.

Felipe Franco
Former Deputy Commissioner Division of Youth and Family Justice, City of New York, Administration for Children's Services
150 William Street, New York, NY 10038

Question: The role of the boards of directors/trustees has changed since the crash of 2008 and the impact of new restrictive governmental regulations. Concomitant to that, have these changes adversely affected the role of the CEO and/or the direction and purpose of your agency?

Felipe Franco: In recent years, as a result of the downturn of the economy, many nonprofit boards have been focusing on fundraising as a prerequisite for a successful CEO. While this is understandable, it does not allow for a focus on fundamentals that leadership must address with respect to inequality in education, housing, and employment.

While it is likely that the government will have fewer resources to distribute in the near term, it is important to develop an active partnership to assure that services are not negatively impacted. We must look for new entrepreneurial opportunities and business models to assure our continued success.

Question: How has your agency responded to the current conversation on diversity, equity and inclusion and the need for anti-racist approaches? How have these conversations affected the sector?

Felipe Franco: No issue is more crucial for government and nonprofit leadership than the concern for social equity, particularly income inequality. ACS has made great strides to redeploy our resources (internally and to the nonprofit sector) from detention to prevention. Our work over the last five years has resulted in a 90% reduction in youth placements in juvenile justice.

Hundreds of Hispanic and African-American children and families are now receiving support in their homes and neighborhoods, instead of unnecessary and ineffective incarceration. We in government must partner with the nonprofit sector to develop multi-generational neighborhood approaches that invest in opportunities to reduce inequality. Issues of diversity and equity must be addressed at all levels of leadership, not only in government but in the nonprofit sector as well.

Authors' Notes:

The intention of the authors is not to be critical of the practice of social work, especially clinical practice but rather to suggest consideration of a combined macro/micro practice theory.

At times, we are prescriptive and at others we suggest not one answer to a specific issue but a number of approaches and solutions.

We are though asking our social work leaders, Deans of Schools of Social Work, scholars, agency leaders and organizational heads to understand that the history of our profession demands not only a focus on societal change but also on activism required to confront todays ills and issues.

In our opinion it is insufficient to address the individual needs and behaviors that afflict our society without addressing the social structure that often is the primary factor that causes human suffering.

Appendix A: NYU Silver's Adaptive Leadership in Human Services Initiative

NYU Silver's Adaptive Leadership in Human Services Initiative was launched in 2016 by Dr. Lausell Bryant and her colleague, Marc Manashil, now an adjunct lecturer at NYU Silver. It consists of curricular and extracurricular activities. Activities are supported by grants from the Katherine & Howard Aibel Family Foundation, the B. Robert Williamson Jr. Foundation, the New York Community Trust and most recently, the Staten Island Foundation. Adaptive leadership is integrated into the macro practice courses for second year students and we have a standing elective for MSW students and a required course for DSW students. There is a stipend and a post-graduate certificate course for nonprofit executives. We have an adaptive leadership community for social work professionals who want to work on common adaptive challenges such as addressing racism in their organizations or other topics.

The learning objectives for adaptive leadership in the graduate social work curriculum include:

1. *Increasing students' understanding of the organizational or community stakeholder systems of which they are a part before taking action;*
2. *Gaining a greater understanding of their roles and behavior so they can interact in organizational and community stakeholder systems more effectively;*
3. *Deepening their experimental mindset to make progress on difficult adaptive challenges;*
4. *Confronting the loss and other forms of resistance that they will face in trying to bring about necessary change; and*
5. *Increasing their resiliency and ability to sustain themselves in the work of change-making for as long as possible.*

Learning outcomes include:

1. *Distinguishing between leadership and authority and how to assess when each is called for;*

2. *Distinguishing between technical and adaptive challenges and examining which aspects of each are present in challenges;*

3. *Becoming more aware of the role they play in groups;*

4. *Identifying a purpose that drives their desire to make change and will sustain them when the going gets tough;*

5. *Learning to conduct a diagnostic of their organizational system and its stakeholders;*

6. *Understanding how individuals and systems respond to the disequilibrium of change;*

7. *Implementing interventions and pacing the work;*

8. *Understanding ways in which we engage in work avoidance; and*

9. *Engaging in critical self-reflection.*

Bibliography

1. DiJulio, C. (2018, April 06). The Washington Post/Kaiser Family Foundation Survey on Political Rallygoing and Activism. Kaiser Family Foundation. www.kff.org/other/report/the-kaiser-familyfoundation-washington-post-survey-on-political-rallygoing-and-activism/

2. Schlegel, R. (2020, March 13). By the Numbers: How Philanthropy Responded During the Great Recession. National Committee for Responsive Philanthropy. https://www.ncrp.org/2020/03/greatrecessionanalysis.html

3. Venkataramani, A. S., Bair, E. F., O'Brien, R. L., & Tsai, A. C. (2019). Association Between Automotive Assembly Plant Closures and Opioid Overdose Mortality in the United States: A Difference-in-Differences Analysis. *JAMA Internal Medicine*, 180(2), 254-262. doi:10.1001/jamainternmed.2019.5686

4. Maitoza R. (2019). Family challenges created by unemployment. *Journal of Family Social Work*, 22(2):187-205. doi:10.1080/10522158.2018.1558430

5. The Anti-Defamation League. (2019). Audit of Antisemitic Incidents 2019. www.adl.org/audit2019

6. Dreyer, B. (2019). Sustained Animus toward Latino Immigrants — Deadly Consequences for Children and Families. *New England Journal of Medicine*, 381(13), 1196-1198. doi: 10.1056/NEJMp1908995

7. Ingraham, C. (2017, December 06). The richest 1 percent now owns more of the country's wealth than at any time in the past 50 years. *The Washington Post*. https://www.washingtonpost.com/news/wonk/wp/2017/12/06/the-richest-1-percent-now-owns-more-of-the-countrys-wealth-than-at-any-time-in-the-past-50-years/

8. Amandolare, S., Bowles, J., Gallagher, L., and Garrett, E. (2020, May). Essential Yet Vulnerable: NYC's Human Services Nonprofits Face Financial Crisis During Pandemic. Center for an Urban Future. nycfuture.org/research/essential-yet-vulnerable

9. Salsberg, E., Quigley, L., Mehfoud, N., Acquaviva, K., Wyche, K., and Sliwa, S. (2017, October). Profile of the Social Work Workforce. Council on Social Work Education. https://www.cswe.org/Centers-Initiatives/Initiatives/National-Workforce-Initiative/SW-Workforce-Book-FINAL-11-08-2017.aspx

10. Burghardt, S., DeSuze, K., Lausell Bryant, L., & Vinjamuri, M. (2017). *A Guide for Sustaining Conversations on Racism, Identity, and our Mutual Humanity. Cognella Academic Publishing.*

11. Heifetz, R.A., Linsky, M., and Grashow, A. (2009). The practice of adaptive leadership: Tools and tactics for changing your organization and the world. Harvard Business Press.

12. Lausell Bryant, L. and Manashil, M. "Adaptive Leadership for Organizational Change." Syllabus, New York University, New York, NY, 2011.

13. Lausell Bryant, L. "Reflections on Change, Risk & Loss," NASW Currents, Summer 2020, Vol 65(1).

14. Baker, E. L., Irwin, R., & Matthews, G. (2020). Thoughts on Adaptive Leadership in a Challenging Time. Journal of Public Health Management and Practice, 26(4), 378-379. doi:10.1097/phh.0000000000001179

15. Erhard, W., Jensen, M.C. & Granger, K.L. (2013). Creating Leaders: An Ontological/Phenomenological Model. Harvard Business School Negotiation, Organizations and Markets Research Papers.

16. McKeever, B. (2018, December 13). The Nonprofit Sector in Brief 2018: Public Charities, Giving, and Volunteering. Urban Institute. https://nccs.urban.org/publication/nonprofit-sector-brief-2018#the-nonprofit-sector-in-brief-2018-public-charites-giving-and-volunteering

17. Diamond, D. (2017, July 17). How hospitals got richer off Obamacare. Politico. https://www.politico.com/interactives/2017/obamacare-non-profit-hospital-taxes/

18. Johnson, C. (2019, February 07). Giant hospital system's charity status challenged. The Washington Post. https://www.washingtonpost.com/health/2019/02/07/giant-hospital-systems-charity-status-challenged/

19. Ramey, C. (2015, July 05). N.J. Hospitals Monitor Effect of Tax-Court Ruling in Morristown. The Wall Street Journal. www.wsj.com/articles/n-j-hospitals-monitoreffects-of-tax-court-ruling-in-morristown-1436145018

20. Ofri, D. (2020, February 20). Why are non-profit hospitals so highly profitable? The New York Times. www.nytimes.com/2020/02/20/opinion/nonprofit-hospitals.html

21. Charity Navigator. (n.d.). Charity Navigator's Methodology. Your Guide To Intelligent Giving. https://www.charitynavigator.org/index.cfm?bay=content.view&cpid=5593

22. Charity Navigator (n.d.). Charity Navigator Encompass Rating System. https://www.charitynavigator.org/index.cfm?bay=content.view&cpid=8077

23. Lausell Bryant, L. (2019). Leadership Development for Social Workers: Fulfilling the Promise of the Profession [Video Tutorial]. SAGE Publications, Ltd.

24. University of Southern California. (n.d.). People of the Academy. USC Sidney Harman Academy for Polymathic Study. polymathic.usc.edu/about/people/sidney-harman